THE ENTREPRENEUR'S BIG BOOK™

ON THE BUS™
Small Business Owners Coaching

THE ENTREPRENEUR'S BIG BOOK™

Featuring the 12 Steps of Entrepreneurship
Supporting Your Entrepreneurial Journey

Chris Lipper

The Entrepreneur's Big Book™
Featuring the 12 Steps of Entrepreneurship
Supporting Your Entrepreneurial Journey

ISBN 978-1-958150-18-4

ON THE BUS™
Small Business Owners Coaching

DEDICATION

To my father, Arthur Lipper III, who will have to agree to disagree with most of this. I have learned more from my dad of what to do than what not to do, but there's been some of that too. Most of all, my dad has taught me to be a connector and he is someone you want on your side. I get a lot of that from him and am grateful.

To my fellow entrepreneurs and inventors – thank you! We are needed. Thank you to everyone who's taken a shot and thinks outside the box and thrives on hearing that it can't be done. Where would we be without some of all the wonderful inventions and innovations in our lives? Thank you!

Much of this book outline was taken from books of recovery. You should know that due to anonymity I can neither confirm nor deny if I am in recovery, let's just assume that I am not. I can tell you that I have seen firsthand the success of books like these countless times and that I can share with you that tools in this book will work if you work them, even for entrepreneurs.

I also want you to know that this book will not be for everyone. We will be discussing spirituality and a God of your understanding. If this is something you are not comfortable with or open to, this book may not be for you. You can water down the message to your own taste, taking what you need and leaving the rest, but you may also get different results then.

While writing this book I have had some great wins!! Some great personal losses!! I got COVID-19, which was awful. Some of what's gotten me through all of that are the entrepreneurial stories included in the book and I am forever grateful to those of you who contributed. Thank you. I am very proud of all of us and this version and later updates of *The Entrepreneur's Big Book™* will change lives!

ACKNOWLEDGEMENTS

I want to thank 100s of entrepreneurs who I've had the privilege and honor to coach over the years. You've allowed me to fine tune my tools and kept me motivated, energized, and interested in life. I hope that I helped you in some way as well. I'd like to thank all the people who have worked with and for me over the years from the early days with Jason Kamps, Barry Jabloner, Judy, Michael, Helen, and Lisa. To the current days with Stephen, Renee, Scott, and Meredith.

I of course must thank my family: Anni, Arthur, Samantha, Victoria, Christina, Randa, Michael, and Ruth for putting up with my ups and downs over the years, I couldn't have done it without your love and support.

I have to, need to, and want to thank the team that helped me with this book. Barry Cohen for encouraging me and moving me along. Marco for the logos and artwork. Nancy Delain, my current lawyer. Most of all, and batting cleanup, Heather Felty, you've done an amazing job and I would recommend you to anyone wanting to go through this process. Thank you all. I am proud of what we created.

Last but not least to all the entrepreneurs who shared their stories in this book inspiring others to be great and to all the entrepreneurs who are going to do great things and be in this edition of *The Entrepreneur's Big Book™*.

Table of Contents

FOREWORD

I have experienced coaching from both sides of the desk. I have seen many of what I call the "pretenders to the throne" – people who had a mid-life crisis, got bored with their job, were downsized or laid off, and decided to take a six-week course, hang out a shingle... and "poof!," they were a coach.

I have also experienced the experts who floated down from their corporate Mount Olympus and attempted to anoint aspiring entrepreneurs with their wisdom. Most of them never had the guts to start and run a business prior to starting their coaching practice.

Chris Lipper is neither of the above. I have had the opportunity to observe what he has created. This book simply codifies an approach that has succeeded for the many business owners who have put their trust in him. Those willing to do the work have succeeded. You will read just a few of their stories in this book.

What Chris has created goes beyond typical one-to-one coaching. He has synthesized the best of one-to-one coaching, peer group counseling, and the mastermind group approach – along with the creation of virtual trade shows and a community of like-minded supportive business owners who are committed to each other's success. And succeed they have.

This book will open your mind to a non-judgmental methodology that combines a little Eastern wisdom with practical common-sense self-examination that every business owner can use at any stage of his or her business. The author follows the tenet of the greatest sales trainer that ever lived – the late, great Zig Ziglar – who said, "You get what you want by helping others get what they want."

Read, profit, and enjoy!

– Barry Cohen, author and editor

INTRODUCTION

What type of entrepreneur are you?

Taught	Dentist
Bought	Optometrist
Ready, fire, aim	Chiropractor
Inherited	Lawyer
Widowed	Contractor
Forced	Hobbyist
Franchisee	Practice
Franchisor	Business owner
Natural	Inventor
Real	Writer
Compulsive	Comedian
Starters	Artist
Giver upper	Mompreneur
Out there	Dadpreneur
Dreamer	Coach
Can't let goer	Trainer
Multi-leveler	CPA
Solopreneur	Bookkeeper...
Doctor	

If you are sending quotes, estimates, and invoices, you are probably an entrepreneur. While anyone in business can benefit from the contents of this book, it was written for my favorite type of entrepreneur: founding entrepreneurs.

I have to be honest with you, writing is not what I do best, and I am kind of writing and editing in-between appointments. With that said, there is probably no one on the planet who understands entrepreneurs of all types as well as I do. I feel a little Trump-like saying that, but it's true. I grew up in a family of entrepreneurs and have been one most of my life. I remember, as a kid, my brother had a skateboarding company selling wheels, bearings, and decks, while I was selling the artwork I'd make in school to my parents' friends.

I remember some pretty impressive entrepreneurs, business owners, and presidents being in our home while I was growing up – from Leonard Stern, Nick Deak, and Leonard Lauder to Dick Fisher and Michael Steinhart. My Dad, Arthur Lipper III, is a world class entrepreneur and these types of people liked being around him and vice versa.

I've seen this firsthand in my life. I do it on a smaller level with small business owners. I think there is an energy we just all enjoy connecting with people. Bottom line, I am not a textpert (someone who just reads a book and considers themselves an expert, without having lived the experience). My life and business experience qualify me to author this book. This is my second book, and I am following a format I enjoy.

The beginning of the book consists of the basic text sharing my story and some of my experiences. The "How It Works" chapter contains the 12 Steps for Entrepreneurs, which I hope becomes the meat of the book with the tools I am suggesting and that you will consider using.

Being an inventor, I have a fondness for inventors, and I think they deserve a special section, so I have included at the end of this book a chapter on inventing, which I believe will help any entrepreneur become better at what they do. It is just some basics to get you started on how to think and mechanics on what to do. I may also release this as a stand-alone pamphlet at a later date.

One of the intentions of this book is that it be used for group discussions in our On The Bus™ meetings as focus of a topic meeting. We will use each chapter and each of the 12 Steps of Entrepreneurship as discussion topics at our meetings. We can share with each other there what we are doing and how it's working.

The middle of the book has different stories from entrepreneurs letting us know where they started, how they and their business has changed, and where they are now. The intent is that this book continues to evolve and to re-release this book with new stories or add to them every few years. Some of the stories will be anonymous and are intended to allow the writers to be honest with the ups and downs of each entrepreneur's experience, strength, and hope.

In their personal stories, the entrepreneurs share what their life and business used to be like, what changes and pivots they've made when joining a group like On The Bus™, and what life and business are like now. The intent is not to say how great On The Bus™ or Chris Lipper are, although it's nice to hear and humbling to know the difference we've made.

The idea is to share entrepreneurs' stories, mistakes, and solutions in a general way.

This book is meant for the already started, the up and coming, and the struggling entrepreneur. For those where life and business are just exactly perfect, this may not be the book for you, but I suspect you will get some value from it regardless.

Being an entrepreneur can be scary, so can driving long distances alone. I am not suggesting that there is anything wrong with it or us. I am also not suggesting that entrepreneurship is a disease and I am certainly not poking fun at anyone in recovery or who's gained in life from similar books. I am just suggesting that entrepreneurship can be a bit of an addiction. Staying focused can be a challenge. Wanting to do it alone may be something at our core – if you want something done right you do it yourself kind of thing. Winning with others is still winning and sure beats losing alone or even winning alone. Get On The Bus™. Let's plot a vision, a destiny of your choosing. Let's stay the course and learn how to pivot if really needed. Learn from others' mistakes. And most of all, enjoy your ride.

Chapter 1
Chris' Story

My name is Chris Lipper and I am an entrepreneur.

Let me just say that I don't believe in gurus and don't want to be one with my books. I have coached and facilitated over a thousand meetings of people sharing challenges and hearing solutions, which does make me have different experiences than most.

I have asked a number of people I've worked with – friends, current clients, and past clients – to share their stories here in a short story format and I'll lead the way with mine. The intent is to gain insight, learn from our mistakes, and gain from our experiences. My aim is to release new stories in a revised version in the years to come.

As I mentioned in the introduction, I grew up in a family of entrepreneurs as far back as I can remember and was surrounded by them. I never knew a different way of living. I just knew there was an energy about these people that I didn't see in others, and I wanted to be like them.

Family vacations were never just to the beach, but more a business trip the kids could come on, which was fine by me. Like many kids, I had odd jobs and also "real" jobs. Though I did have jobs when I was younger and liked them, I did not like having to ask permission to try something in a different way or to follow others' (my bosses) ideas. I did it, but not with the same passion as pursuing my own ideas.

I started my first job when I was 11 years old. I was in boarding school and had very long vacations. My parents were not sure what to do with me, so they got me a job with "Uncle Lee" in the Diamond District in New York City as a runner. I made $20 a day; my mom would send me with lunch and paid for my train ticket to Grand Central Station in New York City. I'd walk a block and a half to 47th Street between 5th and 6th Avenues and made $100 a week cash. I started learning there how to sell. What a great experience from a retail perspective. I learned how to greet people, getting out from behind the counter. I learned to listen for and understand people's buying signals. I also saw how both sides negotiated; it was all fascinating to watch and I loved it.

> **"I learned the power of getting a paycheck**
> **– and that it was better to be the boss."**

After that I worked in the kitchen in my high school boarding school for ARA Food services. I learned how to load an industrial dish washing machine, mop floors, clean pots, and that the smell of spoiled milk in the milk machine smelled something awful. I also learned the power of getting a paycheck every two weeks – and that it was better to be the boss.

Next, I started a handyman company. I was probably 14 and my parents' friends would pay me to fix things and do odd jobs they didn't want to do, like emptying the gutter of leaves.

After that, my next job was with Bob Gintell at Gintell & Company, a financial firm / Mutual fund in Greenwich, CT. I started as a gofer type and ended up spending a lot of time in the trading room. I loved the energy in the trading room – both the stress and the excitement.

Being a big tennis player at the time, on my way to being a USTA Rated 5.5 player at my best, I founded CSL Sports, representing different tennis equipment companies. I remember having a different grip manufactured, strings, and an innovative, patented three-string racket. I'd go from tennis club to tennis club selling the rackets. I learned pretty quickly that if you could get the Pro to use the racket, that the other members would follow. I recognized the power of having others sell for you.

If your business model has distribution channels like stores, salespeople, distributors, or down links, why would you sell directly to consumers? Support your channels of distribution. Rather than sell to individuals, send the individuals to the stores. Most importantly, I saw the power of production. If you are selling more than the company can make, that's a big problem. This work required a ton of driving, so I also learned the importance of making truck routes for your stops. I learned then to create days for office/phone calls and days for selling when I was on the road.

I then went back to college, which in hindsight I realized was never going to work for me. I had just done eight years, including summers, of boarding school. I wanted to get out in the real world.

My dad had an institutional trading firm, New York and Foreign Securities, at the time, so I worked for him, and he made sure I was the lowest paid and hardest working person in the company. We'd leave the house together every morning at 5:45 AM. At 5:46, if I was a minute late, I'd see nothing but brake lights going down the driveway. We would be at work at 805 3rd Avenue in New York City before 7:00 AM. We'd turn on the lights and make coffee every morning. My dad was the boss. We had 50 or so employees, but he was always the first to arrive and the last to leave – every day.

"Entrepreneurship: is it a passion or an addiction?"

Being an entrepreneur can be a bit of an addiction and work life balance can slip away. I remember seeing a picture once of my dad at his desk with a gas mask on. There was a gas leak in the building, and he refused to leave as he was working on something, so the firemen made him put on the mask. I guess I can say the same about myself as I am writing this on Christmas morning, 2021. I am not sure if it's an addiction or more of a passion – a passion that we have some control over. We will talk more about this later.

After getting my Series 7 license on the third try at 20 years old, I left the industrial trading desk that I loved and went down to work on the floor of the NYSE for about a year. I loved it there, too; I found the people there to be funny, fun, and very bright. However, the numbers moved too quickly for me. Buy programs and sell programs were just starting upstairs and we were still writing with manual tickets downstairs. The fear of making a mistake was too high and I lost my first job.

This was the Friday before the Monday crash of 1987. I am not saying that any of us had any insight of what was to come, but the market did crash that Monday. Back then when someone upstairs hit a button there was a rumbling on the floor. You could feel it coming, and then boom, all your phone lights would light up. It was a crazy, crazy time. I remember triple witching days when the tape could run off 400 points the other way, two hours after closing. I remember one day after the market closed up 200 points, going out for drinks, and coming back to see that the market closed down 400 points. They were good times, interesting times.

I left Wall Street then, and have never made an investment since, and have been wrong for 30,000 points waiting for the market to crash. I just don't get why the market is up and holding for so long. But I am happy to be wrong.

I then sold advertising for a bit with *Venture* magazine, another company my dad owned. Same deal; I was expected to be one of the hardest workers and lowest paid employees. It was somewhat of a sinking ship by the time I got there. Great magazine, great people, great subscription base – 450,000 paid circulation of business owners. Everything was great, except when the market crashed. People needed to cut back and the first thing they cut was their advertising. There were a lot of magazines in the space fighting for the same advertising dollars and one needed to go. *Venture* got sold and I moved on to work for *Institutional Investor*. I learned a ton at *Venture*. I had a great boss, James MacDonald, who had us going on at least two appointments a day, 10 a week.

At *Institutional Investor* I was in the Sponsored Conference Division. This magazine had conferences multiple times a year and would sell sponsorships. They were really quite amazing in their day. I learned a lot at *Institutional Investor*. Gil Kaplan, the owner, personally trained us and taught us to get on the other side of the prospect's desk. Unfortunately, the magazine got sold and the division was closed. I was the last to be let go; I think they thought they were doing me a favor, but all my co-workers ran ahead and got the good jobs.

When I was 25, I founded Marketing Plus. This was my second repping company. I was really an employee of several companies but viewed them as my clients who I represented under an umbrella of Marketing Plus. There was a cable TV station where we had still pictures turned into film, a newspaper targeting women, and a company that would place ads on video case covers in local video rental stores. [A thing from the past for you younger folks: when you wanted to watch a movie outside of the cinema or scheduled on HBO/TV, you went to a store, rented a VHS tape copy of the movie for a few days, and returned it re-wound in the box that had local ads on it.] I enjoyed this as

I was able to get to know many of the local retailers and restaurants, but it wasn't sustainable.

I was then asked to work for the world's oldest and largest embroidered emblem company, Lion Brothers. This was very interesting; I was asked to open 7th Avenue in New York City for them. At the time, 7th Avenue was the apparel design mecca. I loved working with a tangible product and creative people. There was something really cool about seeing something you sold and/or helped design in the stores or walking down the street. This was the company where I really got to cut my chops selling. I'd canvas one building a day; I started floor-by-floor in the Empire State Building. I didn't get my first order until the 16th floor. After about a year or so, we'd landed every major brand you could think of: The Gap, Old Navy, DKNY, Reebok, Ralph Lauren, and many more... all from knocking on doors and asking for referrals.

At every job or company that I've had, I always learned something and believed that I was there for a reason, and it was never a waste of time. At Beecker, Glasser, Runsdorf I learned how to greet customers and how people negotiate. On Wall Street, I learned that there is some value to being a good guy and being popular. I learned that you don't have to have a college degree to be successful, and it's very much who you know. In advertising, I learned that numbers talk and bull shit walks. I learned the importance of who you know and how important it is just to get an appointment or in the door.

> *"Most entrepreneurs are unemployable; we need to run with our own ideas."*

Then I started a series of companies: Chris Co. Inc., Lipper Man Ltd., RU Ready Yet, and On The Bus™, where I focused on creating my own products and services. I found my calling and my passion, taking charge of my life and my business. No more worries about getting fired or laid off. Being a compulsive entrepreneur makes me a bad employee. As I tell most entrepreneurs when they sign on with me, "We are unemployable, and I mean that as a compliment." We don't like to wait and ask for permission; we need to run with our own ideas.

The Pride of Inventing: 15 years of Chris Co. Inc.

My first patented idea was for a hang tag in the apparel industry. For those who don't know what a hang tag is, it's the piece of paper or cardboard you cut off and throw away that's attached generally to the neck of a garment, usually with a swift tack – a string-like piece of plastic. What I learned about how the apparel industry works is you take a garment – let's say a T-shirt – that wholesales for five bucks and costs you $2.50 to make. You put a print on it for a buck – now you can sell it for $15. You put a licensed print on it; now you can sell it for $20 or $25. The way the apparel industry works on some levels (not every time and not for everyone) is we're dressing up garments, making them attractive to an audience in order to sell them for more.

I wanted to make a hang tag and I had the idea of incorporating a removable tattoo as a gift with purchase. It was a very inexpensive medium to use but it had a perceived higher value. This was in the early 1990s. Dennis Rodman was a big star and basketball player, and had tattoos all over his body. We weren't seeing this every day back then; this was new for a lot of us. Tattoos became popular and soon we were seeing tattoo images on T-shirts. I figured let's use removable tattoos as a GWP, gift with purchase. That was where that idea came from. Converse® was the first client I wanted as they sponsored Dennis Rodman, so it seemed like a natural fit for us. I can't recall if they were the first client I got. I got them by going from tradeshow to tradeshow and trying to get appointments with them. I remember I chased them from New York to Atlanta to Chicago to Vegas at trade shows. I would try to get appointments with their marketing people, and I couldn't. But I eventually learned the person's name and I found out he was at the show. I remember waiting outside of a bathroom. I saw him go into the bathroom. I had a mock-up I created in my hand. I walked with him back from the bathroom to his booth and I said, "Hi, my name is Chris Lipper and I have something I've wanted to show you." I shook his hand as we walked back to his booth. I put it in his hand, and I said, "These are tattoo hang tags for your Dennis Rodman line." He looked at me and he said, "Of course we're going to do this. Here's who you talk to." Then we were on our way with our first order. Could you say I was an overnight success? I guess if you looked at that day and not the year it took to get there. Not to mention by the time

I got to Vegas I was broke and had to win the money for the hotel on the blackjack table. Entrepreneurs' lives aren't for everyone; they are nerve racking, but very exciting times.

Then we got Keds®, who became my biggest customer. We worked with them on a line of sneaker hang tags called sneaker art, where they used our tattoos and kids could design their own shoes with the supplied images. They were ordering 100 million of these a year. Then we got Skechers®, and then others, and that business grew very nicely.

Then I came up with my next ideas. We were doing tattoo trading cards, tattoo greeting cards, and tattoo cereal boxes, which put us further in the licensing field of opportunities. Nothing really came from this other than a couple of patents and a new line I developed called Cyberwinks that included a patented plush doll. The idea was that people would send a plush doll which would wink, kiss, or frown and could sit on your monitor versus just emailing the emoticon. Next were gemstone tattoos where I got to learn about retail with our own line of gemstone tattoos called Whozy Woozy™, and I kept inventing and continued creating new products. It was exciting. It was ego fulfilling; the phone was ringing.

> *"The mistake I made, which many inventors make, and many entrepreneurs make is that I forgot to focus on what got me here."*

We had a wonderful manufacturing partner in China. Everything I've ever heard about the Chinese, in my opinion, is propaganda. They were the best manufacturers in the world at that time that I could find to work with. As one of my clients explained, I had to manufacture overseas because that's where the garments were coming from, so I needed a manufacturer in China. It didn't make sense to manufacture in the US, have it shipped to China, and then have the garments come back here. We needed a manufacturer in China; we got lucky and found the right one. I reached out to the Chinese Consulate to find a manufacturer. I got a list of 20 manufacturers; four of them had email addresses. This was the early 1990s when everyone else was using faxes. I sent out emails to the four. Two responded, so I started working with these two companies; one surpassed the other and they had a Canadian office as well, so I was able to work with them here in Vancouver in the daytime, and at night in China. It was wonderful.

The mistake I made, which many inventors make, and many entrepreneurs make, is that I forgot to focus on what got me here. I kept creating and inventing because the nature of inventors and entrepreneurs is whatever you're working on becomes the shiny object and that gets your attention and your energy. It's not just time, but it's all your energy that goes into it, so every time I came up with the next idea it got my attention and energy. I took my eye off the ball of what got me there – I continued creating in multiple industries rather than putting my attention on doing more with the Tattoo Hangtags™. In hindsight I should have licensed the Tattoo Hangtags™ to better partners and then moved on to the next products. What I did was licensed them to two publicly traded companies that really didn't do anything with them and moved on to the next products where I didn't do enough with them. I was in creating mode and forgot to be selling at the same time.

Then I came up with the idea of the medicated tattoos, where we were delivering drugs and vitamins;

echinacea, ascorbic acid, and acetaminophen were some of the early ones. The idea was that as the drug or vitamin was delivered in it and the image on the tattoo would change as the drug was delivered. That was huge; it was far bigger than me. I remember when we were starting, being invited by the FDA to apply for what's known as a pre-IND meeting with the FDA. I'm probably the only person you will ever know who has had a pre-IND meeting with the FDA while working from home. I wasn't a pharmaceutical company, I was just an inventor with an idea working out of my basement. I had to remind them of that. I ended up meeting with their 40 guys in white coats. This was in the early 90s, they've got a big screen with my patent drawing on it in Washington, DC. They keep whispering in my ear, we want you to work on fentanyl, we want you to work on fentanyl. I said no, I don't want to work on fentanyl. That's just not my thing. Let me do echinacea, let me do ascorbic acid and acetaminophen, let me just get my feet wet and get into this whole thing. They wanted us in the major leagues right away. All of a sudden, we were having problems at the patent office, which I'd never had in all my years of inventing. I'm not saying that somebody at the FDA talked to someone at the patent office, but

I'm not saying it didn't happen either as my patents were issued worldwide except in the USA.

That ended my inventing days. In my opinion, the patent office is broken. Now I hear it's taking five years to issue a patent that's going to last for 20 years. It's not enough time to do what you need to do. You can't stay pending for five years and try to license something. That's why I decided to start selling the picks and shovels and teaching people how to do this stuff and other ways of protecting the fort than just patents. A huge part is distribution. And nobody views that as intellectual property, but distribution is everything. How do you take an idea from your head to your pocket? A website's not the only answer. Those were good days. Those were fun days. And I feel that's when I was at my best.

I tried to license some of that out to others. We had two publicly traded companies selling for us, which was interesting. I would go to their quarterly meetings on conference calls. One of the companies was located in White Plains, New York, the other in California. They offered me a big job in a corner office, as they put it. They didn't want to buy the product; they wanted me. I am not sure how I would have done there and neither of us pursued it.

While inventing, I joined a wonderful company called The Alternative Board (TAB) and loved it as a member. The owner, a sweet guy who would often have me pinch hit when he couldn't make a meeting, died. So, I bought the franchise from the estate. I had already started On The Bus™ a year or two prior, but TAB was the main focus. We did very well. At one point my franchise was the fastest growing worldwide.

Coaching Franchise / R.U. Ready Yet / On The Bus™
As I mentioned, I had bought a Coaching Franchise that was a peer advisory franchise, which helps small businesses overcome obstacles by sharing solutions with other members. Franchise owners facilitate the meetings. My first new client was the franchise lawyer who oversaw the negotiations and stayed with me for a number of years. She was right. She told me not to do the deal as there wouldn't be enough income to cover franchise fees and my current obligations. What she didn't see or understand was the personal growth I received from being a franchise owner.

So, the jury is still out on my investment. Would I have the knowledge and confidence to write books or guide $20,000,000 companies? Probably not. I only learned those things from facilitating close to 1,000 entrepreneurial peer board meetings. The knowledge I have gained from what to do and what not to do is priceless. For that I am grateful, and for me it was worth the investment, not to mention all the wonderful people I've met along the way, many of whom have shared their stories in this book.

Prior to all of this, I had a tremendous fear of public speaking. I remember going to my first Chamber of Commerce event. There were 200 people in the room, and they passed the microphone around to everyone. All I had to do was stand up and say, "Hi, I'm Chris Lipper from XYZ company" and sit down. I'm telling you, I was sweating buckets as it was getting closer to me. And I'm thinking, how the hell do I get out of here? I don't want to do this. Today, I speak in front of groups of that size, and I have no problem. It goes back to that whole thing – was buying the franchise a mistake? I say no, because I've gotten to grow so much and learn so much, and I wouldn't have had that opportunity had I still been the wallflower I was.

What did I attribute the fear to? That I sucked doing it. I don't suck at it anymore. Part of it is that I was very critical of other speakers. As I've gotten less critical, I've become less critical of myself, as well. But I just wasn't very good. It was the experience of running the franchise that helped me get out of my shell and not be a wallflower.

> **"There's always a benefit and a lesson learned from the mistakes entrepreneurs make."**

As I said, when I was buying the franchise, my lawyer at the time expressed what a mistake it was going to be. In some ways, she was right, but in other ways, she wasn't. And I think the point is, if we're going to identify the mistakes that entrepreneurs make, there's always some benefit. There's always a lesson learned. And the lesson may be what not to do next time. You learn something with each stage, and we get better at something with each stage. We don't always know. I like to say my life is none of my business. I float, I'm going through life, and I'm going to end up where I'm supposed to end up and just keep floating. It's not up to me to decide if a day is a good day or a bad day. I don't know. Maybe I was meant to lose that job so I can move on to the next thing. Or maybe there are happy and sad days. I don't know what the big picture looks like. I just know that each day I plug along and do the best I can. And whatever happens, happens.

This is true with most entrepreneurs. It's not always about a balance sheet that determines good or bad. Writing this book, for example, is taking me months and costing me a small fortune by the time you get it. Is it worth it if no one buys it? I think so. It's been healthy for me. I've gotten to connect with some people who I haven't talked to in years. I've jogged some great memories and I have a feeling this book might have some legs and will be used for decades by up-and-coming entrepreneurs.

How things turn out isn't always our responsibility, the results aren't up to me, but the work is. Easy does it, but do it comes to mind. I don't know if I'm steering the ship or doing the rowing – some days, it's a little of both. I think that I would sell myself short if I stopped here, that's for sure – if I were to think what I'm doing now would be good enough. I don't know what the next 10 years will bring; it feels like it's going to bring a lot more than I've got today. But if life ended today, with all that I've gotten to do, and all that I do, that would be good enough. That's great. I feel that I'm on a path – I'm on a trajectory to do much more. And I look forward to that. So, I'm just going to keep floating.

Besides whatever I've already said, my best advice to somebody thinking about entrepreneurship who hasn't taken the plunge yet is to have a vision; it starts with a vision. And the vision should be from your exit backwards. My vision with this business is to franchise and I am building everything I can to make this business franchisable and working backwards. Every decision I make is towards that goal.

Once you become an entrepreneur, can you ever go back to working for somebody else? Most entrepreneurs are unemployable. It is very hard for a business owner, once you've done this for a little while, to have to ask someone's opinion or permission to proceed with a passion. We're go kind of people; at least I am. I've got an idea and I'm going to run with it. I am already 10 paces ahead. I see where it's going. And I know we've got to do the other parts to get there. But I see where we're going. You look at our virtual trade shows. I knew where we were going from day one. We're finally getting there, and I love it. I just need technology to catch up.

> *"As an entrepreneur, you overcome roadblocks by blasting through them."*

How do you overcome the roadblocks as an entrepreneur? You blast through them; you don't go around them. You try to pick up support along the way. But sometimes with entrepreneurs and inventors, the motivator could be when people say no. It's kind of like, "Yeah, I'll show you."

How about the importance of listening to good advice? Mentorship? Not all entrepreneurs can do it. They're blinded by their passion; they're blinded by their vision. In hindsight, maybe it's a good idea at the time, but they're in go mode. I don't view myself as a mentor or a guru, but more that I have put together a community of people. If one person says, no, no, no, you shouldn't do that, you move them out of the way and you go for it. But if you're in a group, like my groups, where there are seven or eight people saying, no, no, no, you shouldn't do that and here's why, here's my experience. You don't want to go this way. These aren't your strengths and you need to focus on what you're good at. Then you listen. Some entrepreneurs will do it their way anyway. But it's different when it comes from a community. And tough love is still love, right? They may hit you in the head and say knock it off. You know, you're in the IT business, why all of a sudden are you in the sheetrock business? This isn't what you do; sub it out.

The greatest gift that I've been able to give to people is the opportunity to be vulnerable, the opportunity to be wrong. The opportunity to have a forum to say I don't know. It's okay. We don't find this everywhere.

"I get to live vicariously through their success. And there's nothing better for me."

The growth I get to see is amazing. This year I had somebody come to me who all of a sudden landed 300 solar panel projects. It resulted from confidence. We just had somebody who came to us definitely down and out. They stumbled into a business sideways, figured out that their technology could get scans of buildings. Just yesterday, I got a call that they landed a $5 million job, the biggest project in their history. It's because they had the confidence *and* they had their systems in place; they were building along the way, and they were ready. Ready is the right word. I can give an hour long talk on the difference between being willing and ready. Everyone's willing to take on a $5 million new client or your biggest client. But who's ready? Ready means you have the capacity, the team, and you have the systems. Those are the big ones for me. That's why I do what I do. I get to live vicariously through their success. And there's nothing better for me.

As for me, I think I'm still getting ready. I am really focused on a new shiny object – building virtual cities. I want more than just virtual trade shows at this point. I plan on launching virtual cities with a release at about the time this book will come out. Yes, I am piling more ideas on again, but that's what keeps me happy – always creating. It's a fascinating time in my life and I'm just forging forward, while floating along. I might need a Chris in my life. I have a vision that I'm building towards and we're getting close. We're very close. Now I am ready to start the process of getting ready to be franchisable. That's probably a year and a half away, but we're getting there. Am I ready personally? 100%. I have the skills, the talent, and I can build the team. What I don't have is the financing. But I've never worried about that before. I've always figured it out.

Chapter 2
There is a Solution

Many business owners come to me one of two ways and I had one of each today. They are stuck and unhappy about their business; they don't like where they've ended up and aren't happy about where they are going. Or they are in the very beginnings of having an idea; they are just getting started and don't want to make a mistake that will affect them years from now.

First, we need a rudder. I find that most entrepreneurs are somewhat rudderless when they come to me. They tend to go where the business is; they started with an idea or service without really thinking it through all the way to the exit. This is fine in the beginning, but in the end, you'll end up coming to a guy like me as you'll find yourself in a business that you no longer love and want to get out of. Your company is no longer what you had envisioned, but you really didn't have a vision, so let's get one if you don't have one now.

What I do is take people through a meditation to the point of exit if they can get there; some can't. We figure out how old they will be when they will exit, where they will be living, who they are living with, and even the car they are driving. We will of course go to their office mentally and see who's there and if the staffing is right to support their lifestyle. We will also determine if we have the right people in the right seats to support this stage of the company's growth and if the business can support the staff, and the staff can support the business. I'll then start dialing back the image five years at a time, focusing on the organization chart until the current day. We will look at behavior goals, checking in with Chapter 11 in the *On The Bus™ WorkBook* and a talk I give twice a year in June and December.

Once we know a vision, let's let others know what the vision is that we are building, and what it is that we are not building, and who we want to work with, and who we don't. As my mother always said, "A fish rots from the head." Let's not be that fish.

Once we have a vision, we need to figure out behavioral goals to get us there. Document them, track them, and be held accountable to make changes. This is all part of what we do On The Bus™.

We have our owners fill out monthly Bus Passes; see a basic example here.

Refer to Step 10 of the 12 Steps of Entrepreneurship later in this chapter. Numbers are all part of having S.M.A.R.T. goals – making goals trackable. To repeat, you should have a vision as to where you are going. Have a rudder. Figure out when you want to exit the business and work it backwards. For example, I am 58 years old. If I want to work until I am 80, then that gives me about 20 more years, allowing for two years to sell the business. I better get cracking. I'd like to have franchises with an On The Bus™ in each state. This book and my previous book, *On The Bus™ WorkBook*, will be a big part of that. What are you doing to make your business sellable, franchisable, or are you just going to let it die on the vine? I'll give you a hint and entrepreneurs hate to hear this: the less of you, the more the company is worth.

> ### *"The less of you, the more the company is worth."*

How do we do that? Systems! You need to have systems in place and manage systems versus people. Your job is to find the people who can work in your systems. As Jim Collins wrote in the book *Good To Great*, "You need to have the right people in the right seats ON THE BUS." Yes, that's where the name of my company came from.

Let's start with organizational charts for today and of my company 20 years from now. As someone said in a meeting recently, you need to manage the spaghetti. Meaning your people need to know who they are reporting to and who the reportees are reporting to and so on.

They also need to know their own behavioral goals so they know if they are having a good day, week, month, quarter, or year. If they are doing all aspects of the business well and can even fire themselves or at least know that it's coming if they can't work within the system for their position.

Build your team. Where you don't have people yet, create job descriptions and start interviewing. Always be interviewing. Even when the position is filled, keep interviewing. It's healthy for everyone to know that you are always looking for talent and improving the team with bench strength.

For solopreneurs, please think how you can use your vendors better. How can some of your vendors help with the roles you need filled? Then put them on your organizational chart. For example, if you have a dynamite bookkeeper, he or she could take the role of the CFO. On your organizational chart, you could write CFO, but it's really your bookkeeper who acts that part for now. If you need a graphic artist, you may not have a graphic artist, but you may have a web developer who's done your website; that person could also do graphics or maybe they have a graphics person on their team, and you can use them in that role. Anyone who is not you who is doing the work provides an opportunity to delegate work so you can get other things done. Logistics people can make great allies for helping you develop production flow systems.

12 Steps of Getting into the Starting Blocks

Before we get into the 12 Steps of Entrepreneurship, let's focus on getting your business started. Following are 12 helpful steps.

First let's make sure you have a business and not just a hobby you are being paid for. Some people get offended by this, so I'll use me as an example. I film bands and get paid for doing it, sometimes. Is it a business? No, it's a hobby that I get paid for. If I do some of the things listed below, maybe it's a business. For me it's just fun and keeps me out of trouble. It's a lot of work, always updating equipment, software, and knowledge so I don't mind getting paid for it when I can, but it's not a business. Is yours? Could it be? Are you willing to do the work?

1. Build your team on your bus. Branding. Distribution.

Let's plan on being franchisable, even if it's not on your radar. Franchises are great at systematizing. One of my favorite business books, which I am way overdue for a re-read, is *The E-Myth*® by Michel Gerber, which is all about the importance of managing systems versus people. Do that. Then you just need to worry about finding the people who can work within your systems, or, even better, make that a system too. Let's take a look at how this works. If you go to McDonald's, every franchise makes french fries the same way. They push a button, put the basket in the oil, the alarm goes off, and they take the fries out. They're made perfectly every time; they have the right mixture of salt and whatever else they put on their fries and get all their potatoes from the same place. I am sure there are some variations here, but there is a system in place to make the fries the same each time. You know they're consistent. As for the managing people part of that, it's just getting them to show up and follow the instructions or the system. So, your job is just to get people who can work within the system. In that scenario, that's the dumbed down version. But that's kind of what managing systems does; it makes it easy for anyone to be successful. And that includes yourself.

Know what you don't do well, and how you can overcome it – whether it's using people, employees, vendors, and/or collaborators. I know I don't write well, so I need to either do a lot of writing, get into a grove to stick with it, basically power through it, and have a team to help edit (thank you team). As I noted in the previous chapter, I used to not speak well. I had a great fear of public speaking; I was petrified to just say my name and company name because I didn't want to focus on myself. Today, I speak pretty well. I've learned how to do this. I'm not saying I've mastered it, but I'm comfortable with it. Just because I do it a lot, I powered through since it became important to the role that I play.

Build your team on your bus. Create branding that makes sense and develop profitable distribution channels.

2. Stay excited, love Mondays.

The non-entrepreneur can't wait for the weekend; the entrepreneur can't wait to start his or her work week because he or she loves what they do and they have a hard time turning it off. I am writing this on a beautiful Sunday afternoon – then again, it's my last day of COVID quarantining. Many entrepreneurs really don't know what day it is when it comes to work. I remember when I was inventing, I was sleeping with a Palm Treo® (one of the first smartphones) so I could check emails from China and confirm graphics in the middle of the night. I can tell you that many entrepreneurs work on doing specific work on Sundays – writing blogs, doing billing, etc. – in my case, watching entrepreneurial biographies on the

History Channel. I love them. It's like sports for me to watch this and shows like *Shark Tank®*.

3. Know what scratches your itch.

Money, creativity, helping people, organizing, motivating. I feel like I've said this before. Money exclusively isn't the only motivation for entrepreneurs. With employees it's typically reward, responsibility, or recognition. For entrepreneurs it's a little different. My why is igniting other entrepreneurs' passion; I am over-the-top passionate about entrepreneurs' passion. I find it to be contagious, I fall in love with them, their passion, their energy, their products, and their drive. I just love the vision and excitement. I love connecting people. When I play hockey, I am a much better assist person than a goal scorer. It's the same thing in business. I just love setting people up for success. That's what scratches my itch. Do I make money doing it? Yes, but it's not the reason why I do it. Service is important to me, and I have found a way of aligning my life, getting paid by helping people I love, and that's why it doesn't feel like work. Know where your ideas come from and have a system as to how you get them and how to evaluate them.

4. An entrepreneur's inventory is our time and energy.

How are you spending your time and more importantly your energy? What should entrepreneurs be spending their time on, and their energy? That depends on the business. I like to have core values or core areas where they can spend their time. So, it could be on developing their products. It could be on developing their team. It could be on working smarter and knowing where to spend the energy and also knowing what time of day is the best time to use a certain energy. I know for me if I have a late lunch and I'm hungry, that meeting right before lunch is probably my best meeting of the day. If I can schedule a sales opportunity to meet with a prospect, that time would make the most sense. We need to know our own energetic flow. I'm not great early in the morning. At the end of the day, I'm kind of shot.

5. Manage workflow systems.

Have an order of events as to how things go out the door. You have to know what happens from the order to the invoice to delivery to the customer – and everything in between. It's nice if there's a way for people to double check each other along the way. With a workflow chart, you can see where the bottlenecks are. It bears repeating: you need to manage systems, not people – and find people who can work within your systems. If not, chaos ensues and will negatively impact your business. When you don't have a workflow system, first of all, you don't know where the bottlenecks are. You probably have some people doing more of the work and some people doing less of the work. If you have a business that can work with assembly lines, you're way ahead of the curve.

6. Getting paid.

For younger companies cash flow can be a problem. Getting paid is pretty important and it's nice when it's timely. Look at your terms. We worked with a construction type company some years ago whose terms were ⅓ at signing, ⅓ when starting the job, and ⅓ at completion. As you can imagine the last ⅓ was the hardest to get. I got them to change their terms to ½ up front and ½ when they started the job, which worked better for them. Also, you never want to accept deposits. Always ask for prepayment. Deposits are refundable, prepayments aren't. They are prepaying for your time, not just materials. Remember, for many of you, your time is your inventory – use it wisely. We also had a client with terms like paid if paid, which is tough if you don't have ongoing work. So when some invoice became a year old he'd send a copy of the invoice with a birthday card to the owner.

We had one client who complained his invoices were not getting paid. He also felt he should fire his receptionist because she wasn't doing anything. We offered a solution: put the receptionist on collections. She was getting seven and eight out of 10 invoices paid compared to his previous five out of 10. The reason was because she could say, "Hey, my boss is all over me, can you get this paid?" It was a receivable person talking to a payables person, and they spoke the same language versus an owner calling. It worked. She is now a key employee, and his collections are greatly improved. The job isn't done until we are paid. For many of us the way it's supposed to work is taking a concept from our head to our pocket so let's not forget the last three feet to our pockets. Chasing money can be awkward. It is for me. I find it very hard to coach clients and then have to chase them for money. Another technique I've found useful is to get the last month's payment up front. So, if I sign a new member for let's say $1,000 a month, their first payment to me will be for $2,000. This is for both their first and last month up front. I have a 30-day cancellation policy, no big contract, but they do pay the last month up front and can come to their last meetings after resigning to say goodbye if they like.

7. Cash flow.

You need to create a stream of recurring revenue. Create something you can build on, so you don't start each year or each month with zero sales. I am not a fan of the one and done model. Some businesses like professional practices are stuck with this. I prefer a subscription model when possible. Perhaps your business can add a subscription product or service. Remember that deposits are refundable; prepayments aren't. Your clients are prepaying for your time. They book time with you, and you may need materials, both of which can't be re-sold, so it's a prepayment. I hope that helps you.

8. Your rope is longer than you may think.

Have a vision, stick with it, put a knot in the end of your rope so you can hang on. Sometimes you have to wait for the right break and be in the right place at the right time by doing the right thing. I caught that break with the On the Bus™ Virtual Trade Shows™ technology. I've caught many other breaks; the idea of this book was a break. Part of my vision is knowing that I'll come up with additional products and ideas allowing for that. I've also been fortunate to have people who believe in me and what I am doing, allowing me to pile on the debt to keep things going. I don't borrow money anymore and now the stars have lined up for me and we are on our way. I wish I knew back in the Med-Tats™ days what I know now. I never should have stopped, and now I have to live with that. I won't do that again, but then again I don't have the same pressures of raising small children and can now take more of a shot, having more knowledge and energy to grow with.

9. There's a difference between the adjective of being entrepreneurial and the noun of being an entrepreneur.

A lot of times people talk about being entrepreneurial. That's the verb, that's having a job and maybe people give you enough rope with which to hang yourself. Being an entrepreneur is different. It's taking all the risk. It's burning your ships, that's no turning back. Many small business owners try to do it halfway. They hold on to their day jobs and I always tell them you can't get to second base with your foot on first base. You need to let go and go for it. I remember one of our members years ago, let's call her Rachel. She had a great job with a huge non-profit in their marketing department and was starting to moonlight. They were doing their best to keep her, letting her know how expensive the licenses were for the software and other tools she was using. I finally convinced her to leave and she got them as a client, paying her more than they were paying as an employee. She went from being entrepreneurial to being an entrepreneur with that move.

"If you've ever sold your Rolex® to stay in business another month, you may be one of us."

I know a lot of people who take over companies and run them beautifully, but they don't have a creative or entrepreneurial bone in their body. They are technicians. They just have different motivators. They are motivated by not screwing it up, maintenance, and growth. They are more of a president and could be just as happy running any large corporation. So, let's explain what it means to be a creative entrepreneur.

I am a creative entrepreneur. What that means is that ideas come to me at perhaps unusual times. They will come to me when I'm in a tired state; it could be if I wake up in the middle of the night, before going to sleep, or when waking up. But it can also happen when I'm driving or in the shower. It's when I'm doing routine things that, all of a sudden, ideas come in. It can also happen when I'm in a difficult situation, where I need to think my way out of something, when new products pop up, new ideas. For me, and I suspect for other creative types, it takes very little to take the focus off of one situation and put it on to something else that is creative and fun. Because that's what we enjoy doing. And that's what we're good at – making that next thing. We're not so good at some of the other stuff. As for the technician, they're great at being a franchisee; they're great at not thinking out of the box, and they're great at getting the job done. They may be wonderful and successful. They're just not as creative. The way creative people work is, sometimes, unfortunately, they tend to be focused on the next thing. It can be the shiny object syndrome. The next thing is always the shiny thing. And sometimes we can forget what got us to a place where we have the luxury to create new things. In my case, being a past inventor, I lost track of the fact that it was one of my early inventions that got me to a place where I could continue inventing, and could afford to do it, and I lost focus of what got me there. I think that's typical. Creative types like to create; we don't like to do.

10. Find motivators.

Review history. Watch the History Channel, with its rags to riches stories. This is one of my favorites to inspire a flash of genius. For me, I just love some of the stories we have available to us. Sunday nights on the History Channel is one for me with all those wonderful stories of people who were told something couldn't be done and they bet it all, proving their critics wrong. If you want to be motivated, watch the story on Heinz® Ketchup, Hershey®, or C.W. Post – what a forward thinking rockstar Marjorie Merriweather Post was! If you love to read, read biographies or business books. Find inspiration from others through learning how they tick, too.

11. That's what being an entrepreneur is – a way of living, not a way of making a living.

It's in our blood if you are a real entrepreneur, a founding type. I don't know if it is just me, or all of us, but I got this idea in my sleep, started working on it right away, writing it down while still in my underwear, un-showered, without any morning meditations (very unlike me, but I think very entrepreneurially). Trust that you are like this for a reason. Take time to reflect on how you want to serve others through your creative spirit. Hell, I am writing this book the only night my favorite band is playing locally, by choice, sorry DSO peeps, but this needs to get done.

12. Some days you just need to reboot.

Not every day is going to be aces, but then again, we never know what a good day or a bad day is. Some days we can just feel a little flat. Reboot your day. Get out, go for a walk, help someone, do something to snap yourself out of it if you're not primed for a good day. Just to elaborate a bit, sometimes the day goes askew, we just need to reboot ourselves. I've had to reboot my computer twice today already. I'm working with new cameras and new other things, and they're not playing nice, so I've had to reboot my technology. That's a chance for the computer to reset.

Sometimes we need to do the same thing ourselves; sometimes our days go a little bit strange. And maybe we need to just go out for a cup of coffee or go for a walk, or whatever rituals we might have in the mornings, if it's a meditative thing, or a prayer thing, that gives us a chance to reboot. I remember when I was very young in business and working from home. I'd rather play video games or do something other than work. So, what I had to do was physically leave the house, walk up to the corner, buy a cup of coffee, and walk back in. I'd wear a jacket and tie even though I was working from home – come to think of it I still wear a dress jacket even though I am working from home post-pandemic. It's a mindset thing. And I needed that mindset. It's a great discipline to start. What happens next for many of us is that we then need the discipline to stop and find that work life balance again.

I think for people who are selling, it could have to do with rejection. It could have to do with fear. It could have to do with being misunderstood, or a misunderstanding. It's our own mindset, but it can ruin a day, a week, a month, a relationship. We need to get centered and reboot, so we don't get stuck in a groove or blow up a situation for the rest of the day. It could cost you a relationship with a client, an employee, a lot of people.

"The real entrepreneur – and I don't mean that in a negative way toward the others – has an uncontrollable need to create, a need to sell… It's generally not about money; there tends to be a greater cause that we get blinded by."

We mentioned the other types of entrepreneurs – ones who inherit companies, multigenerational entrepreneurs, and others who buy companies. I just don't think it's the same. I think the real entrepreneur – and I don't mean that in a negative way toward the others – has an uncontrollable need to create, a need to sell, a need for the doing aspect of it. It's generally not about money for us. Personally speaking, it sure would be nice if it were, but there tends to be a greater cause that we get blinded by.

Chapter 3
How it Works

How it works...

Rarely have we seen an entrepreneur fail who has thoroughly followed our path. That means that somebody has blazed this trail ahead of us. The idea may be unique, but the business model probably isn't. So, there's probably a path. We beg of you to be completely honest with yourself and us. Don't tell us how great you are by boasting; let us know what you need help with, be vulnerable. Please don't tell us what you just did; let us know where we can guide you. Don't just report to us; it doesn't work like that.

> *"Creating and entrepreneurship can be a bit of an addiction."*

I don't think there is anything wrong with entrepreneurship, or with 12 Step programs. There is some useful information there. That said, let's view entrepreneurship as a 12 Step program.

This book may appear to suggest that all entrepreneurs struggle, not at all. What I am suggesting is that it's not always a smooth ride and we do need tools and these are tools for the long haul, not just in the beginning days. These are the tools that can straighten out your ride, keep you going, serve as your GPS, and become your guard rails on your journey. You don't have to do it alone and are probably better off not doing it alone.

12 Steps of Entrepreneurship

Entrepreneurship can be an addiction.

The following is of course borrowed from 12 Step programs and adapted for our purposes. It's meant to be a little tongue in cheek, but it does work.

12 Steps of Entrepreneurship©

1. We admitted that we were powerless over our entrepreneurism - that it makes our lives unmanageable. *Establish a vision of who we want to be and where we are going when we are done.*

2. Came to believe that a community of business owners could restore us to sanity. *Be honest with your community and do the work.*

3. Made a decision to turn our will and our lives over to the care of something bigger than ourselves and *establish behavioral goals.*

4. Made a searching and fearless moral inventory of what makes us tick, the mistakes we have made, and how to get (back) on the right path by *tracking behavioral goals.*

5. Shared the inventory with a mentor and group. *Be held accountable to living your behavioral goals.*

6. Became entirely ready to change, focus, or pivot.

7. Humbly asked for help. *Make the change or dig in for the long haul.*

8. Made a list of all the people we have harmed and mistakes we have made. *Become willing to clean up the mess.*

9. Made attempts to correct our past mistakes and/or learn from them. *Clean up the mess.*

10. Continued to take personal inventory, and when we were wrong promptly admit it. *Staying current with your behavioral goals.*

11. Sought through prayer, meditation, and managing systems to improve our conscious contact. *Keep your vision. Keep your vision growing.*

12. Having had success with THESE steps we try to carry THIS messages to other entrepreneurs and to continue practicing these principles in all our affairs. *Give back to others what we've learned in groups like this. Help others!*

*this is available for download at www.onthebus.biz

1. We admitted that we were powerless over our entrepreneurism – that it makes our lives unmanageable. *Establish a vision of who we want to be and where we are going when we are done.*

Entrepreneurism isn't a bad thing; we just need to know who we are. It is important to understand why we think the way we think and be aware of it. We are entrepreneurs and, for the most part, unemployable, meaning we have a real hard time asking permission and corporations really don't want to hire entrepreneurs as we are hard to manage. Take that all as a compliment; just focus and be careful of shiny object syndrome. You don't have to act on every idea that you have. Save some ideas in a "Not for today" file that you may or may not get to someday. I find by writing things out they're easier to let go of as they aren't rattling around in my head, taking up space and energy.

Here is a suggestion. Think of your life like a wagon wheel with a cog in the middle and spokes coming out of it. The length of the spokes and time slices symbolizes how much of your time and energy you put into each of them. Here is one I made recently.

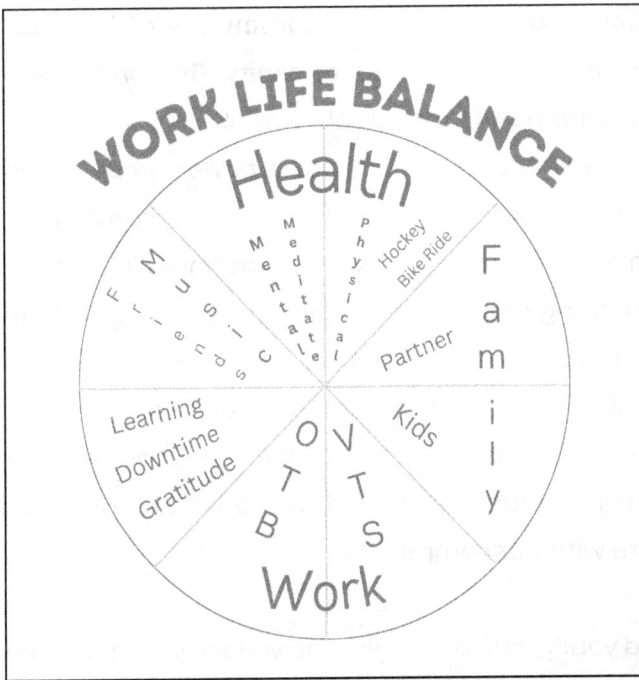

You can play with the length and widths as a goal versus reality if you like. But if the spokes aren't even, the wheel won't turn evenly and it will be a pretty bumpy ride. If I were to update it now, business and music would be larger than, let's say, family and fun, and I will likely adjust that in the next few days. Balance is hard for entrepreneurs and that's why the inventory steps are important. Establish a vision. Know where and when you want to be when exiting the business. Know what that looks like.

2. Came to believe that a community of business owners could restore us to sanity. *Be honest with your community and do the work.*

The traditional 12 Steps state a power greater than ourselves. For entrepreneurs, that power is community. Coming together with others in business is a power, something bigger than you. It is the power of a group that supports you to be a better entrepreneur. The On The Bus™ members in our community do very, very well. It really has little to do with me (as you will hear from their stories included in the book), but much more with our community.

Find your group of people who you are going to listen to and who you can't manipulate. It could be one of the many community-based coaching companies out there, including mine – we are virtual and like our format best – but check others like TAB, Vistage, NIA. Stop running alone, unless it's working for you. My favorite question is: what's it costing you to not be On The Bus™?

Join a group of entrepreneurs, a peer group, or a Mastermind that has regular meetings. Even if you join an association group within your industry it's something. I prefer getting perspective from other industries to help inform my own business. Join a group that works with and understands entrepreneurs. Only entrepreneurs understand entrepreneurs. Stop wasting your time and money with textperts who don't get it and don't get us, as they have their own objectives – which is typically to get you to keep paying month after month. Stick with other owners who are in the trenches every day like you are and are succeeding. Listen to them. Learn from their mistakes.

Going to meetings with like-minded people is helpful. Not all your ideas are going to be great, and being part of a group gives you a place to share your ideas. This is a fellowship thing, a community thing, not a God thing. Your group will give you feedback, and that's what fuels your ability to stretch and grow beyond doing it alone. There is power in community. Remember that Einstein said, "Insanity is doing something over and over expecting a different result;" entrepreneurs expect something to go a particular way, and try it anyway.

Once you are in a group, use it wisely. I am more about saving ass than saving face. You aren't going to *look* good; you are going to *be* good. Go to your meetings prepared. At On The Bus™ we have our members fill out a monthly Bus Pass to prepare for the meeting. They look at their numbers, KPIs, their behavioral goals, receivables, and more, so they know what challenge to present at the meeting. If you want better answers, ask better questions! Please implement when you are given feedback from your group; you know what you should do. Don't just grin and nod and do nothing with the information. Remember the power.

If you are a member of a group, and you are paying the organization, the other members' objective is to help you and that's it. When needed, they will give you tough love, between the eyes sometimes, but it's still love and is meant to be helpful. How you receive it is on you. The best business owners I know understand how to receive and implement feedback. A coach's goal is really to prolong the monthly relationship with you. After the first year, you've gotten what you're going to get from a coach, myself included.

There will always be other ways to do business. Others have done it already and have been successful. Others have failed. These mistakes were made for you to learn and grow. Make a decision to explore/learn about other people's businesses. Learn from others' mistakes so you don't have to make them yourself.

If you are joining a group that is franchised, be a little careful of the franchise owner and franchise management. Remember, a fish rots from the head and if your facilitator is a corporate guy/gal or the guy/gal running the organization, they have no firsthand experience at taking a risk. How can they coach entrepreneurs? How can they understand the passion, the drive, the need to create, and make a difference if they've always had a job? How can you describe or teach someone to swim if you've never done it?

Bottom line, we learn by saying "I don't know" versus coming to a group being a blow hard with all the answers. We will like you a lot more and want to help you if you can just let your guard down and be honest. When you can admit your mistakes and that you don't know, you'll always grow more.

Establish S.M.A.R.T. goals and base your Behavioral Goals to achieve them.

3. Made a decision to turn our lives over to the care of something bigger than ourselves and *establish behavioral goals.*

This might be nearly impossible for some of you. We are egomaniacs and control freaks; it's just part of who we are. In business we need to be able to trust our gut, but also recognize that there is a higher power that connects you to that feeling. When you can turn your will and your life over to that higher power – and know it is *not* you – you see that you can't conquer the world alone. Find something you can believe in. It could be the spirit of Ben Franklin or a God of your understanding – whatever works for you. Ideally you will feel that someone or something is looking out for you, guiding and encouraging you. I use some of the people in my life who have passed away, looking down on me, and make sure I am doing them proud.

We all need a little luck; we all need dots connected that we can't connect on our own. We all need parking spots to open at times or to catch yellow lights before turning red. What I am suggesting here is that we realize we are meant to catch the red light sometimes. Maybe we aren't meant to act on every decision we make and maybe lights happen for a reason we don't know about, like the 18-wheeler that would have hit us down the road. Follow the signs now and you'll understand it later and be glad that you did. This third step is now a verb in my life. I can float with the current versus always trying to swim upstream against it. You know when things are flowing, so flow with it. You also know when you're fighting it and trying to manipulate it. Just flow... And also thank that higher power for guiding you in the right direction. Be in touch with yours.

4. Made a searching and fearless moral inventory of what makes us tick, the mistakes we have made, and how to get (back) on the right path by *tracking behavioral goals.*

Let's take an honest look at ourselves here and confirm that we are true entrepreneurs and building something for the future that we're committed to. Be ready to burn the ships and acknowledge that this isn't just a hobby. Taking an inventory of what has worked – and what hasn't worked – in business in the past. With an inventory in hand, we can move forward making better decisions.

Be careful of N.I.H., Not Invented Here Syndrome. Sometimes you can get great ideas, or the beginning of great ideas, from other people. They may have a slightly different spin or angle on what you are doing. Don't be so quick to dismiss it and maybe take a look in your inventory to ensure that you aren't suffering from N.I.H. Not everything has to be completely original from you.

Only an entrepreneur knows if they have a good day or a bad day. You don't necessarily have to make a sale for it to be a good day. You may have a great meeting that could result in something big later on.

Knowing what makes us tick, knowing our inventory, our bandwidth, is what we share with a coach in the next Step. It is important to research and read/ watch other entrepreneurs' stories. Ted Talks and documentaries can be great motivators. Not just to see how someone else did it, but to know we are not alone. And to help you understand what it is about what you are doing that lights you up, that keeps you working so hard to achieve your goals. We aren't the only ones who have these crazy ideas.

If someone questions if something can really be done, I'm all in. Especially if you tell me it *can't* be done.

Sharing your ideas with others is invaluable as an entrepreneur, especially for solopreneurs. One *can* work alone, but to operate effectively we have to share and get feedback on our processes, our procedures, and our goals. Such critical feedback can't be from employees (who can be fired), it needs to be from peers who can tell us *not* to do things – people who can say, "That's crazy!" Critical feedback is what takes you to the next level up and provides you with accountability to keep you moving along.

5. Shared the inventory with a mentor and group. *Be held accountable to living your behavioral goals.*
Step 4 helped you reflect on your past by making an inventory. Step 5 is when you find a mentor or coach with whom you can share this inventory and who

will help you stay the course. This is someone you're going to feel accountable to – and maybe be a little afraid of them through respect – someone you will listen to and tell everything. If done right, you will feel like you have a clean slate and a new beginning.

As you share your inventory, you will see the patterns of past behavior and be able to modify them to make fewer mistakes in the future. A coach or mentor will also help you recognize when you can benefit from a different approach. They can also point out the things you won't do as much as you'd like to.

When you share honestly with a mentor, they can learn to know you better than you know yourself. When done right, they can even lead us, letting us think that the ideas of what we do or don't do were our ideas guiding us. Always be honest with your advisors; otherwise why have them? We aren't trying to look good here, we are being good. Trust that your coach or mentor has your best interest at heart when they challenge you to push yourself outside your comfort zone. You are paying them to improve yourself and your business. Tough love is still love.

Entrepreneurs know ourselves pretty well. We can be very consistent in where we might wimp out or maybe where we take a shot and shouldn't be so brave. If we can just pause long enough to run the idea by someone and they can reference a recent endeavor or, as I do, remind them of their vision, perhaps a better decision can be made. Perhaps...

6. Became entirely ready to change, focus, or pivot. Change is inevitable. Stay entirely ready to shift, pivot, and at times reinvent; remember that good is the enemy of great. Don't settle for just being good enough. This is important as entrepreneurs mature. We can forget what we were striving for and settle for good enough, where our goal becomes to just not blow it.

Every day is a new day, and every day we get new opportunities. Some days we just need to be grateful for the opportunities, that we are in the right place at the right time and make the most of them. Stop focusing on what you think you deserve or desire and be grateful for what you have. If you are stuck in what it was or what you think it *should* be, you can't move forward.

Be grateful for the cup. You know the saying is the cup half full or half empty, I am grateful for the cup and the opportunities.

One of my favorite coaching moments is when a member gets a new office. It's a chance for new beginnings. You can say that's not who we are anymore, and we don't do things that way anymore. This is who we are now. If you aren't getting a new office anytime soon, maybe paint or redecorate, giving you a new beginning. If we see something that we know needs to be done, but we're not ready to do it, we just kind of wallow along and we're going to die. Change or your company will die. This is your wake-up call.

Being ready to change is when you can grow – in business and in life. We can't stay still, we need to grow and keep evolving. In order to become ready to change, we have to focus on what we want, and completing what we've already started, and not get stuck by doing the same thing over and over.

When we constantly start the next project/idea, we stretch ourselves too thin. Are you spending your time wisely? This is part of the inventory. In order to evolve to the next level you must be ready to change, because you can't grow when you're hitting your head against the wall for the millionth time.

I once had an owner call me up to meet and wanted to meet in a diner. He had a successful company, with seven employees who were like family to him, doing $1,000,000 a year in sales and he kept telling me how great everything was, with his boat and second home in Florida. After an hour of hearing how great everything was, and knowing that generally at this point in a conversation this where there would be an indication of some pain or fear, I asked him, "If everything is so great, why am I here and why are we meeting in a diner instead of your office?"

He paused and his eyes welled up. He slammed his fist on the table and the silverware jumped. He said, "The problem is we aren't growing; we're just maintaining at $1,000,000 in revenue and it can no longer support our team. So either I make a change or I have to let someone go. I've never let someone go before and don't want to do that. These people are like family, I need your help."

In that moment he was ready, he was ready to change or die, as the expression goes. As a coach you have to jump on this moment, this is when they are more teachable and coachable and *ready, not just willing*.

7. Humbly asked for help. *Make the change or dig in for the long haul.*

Please stay humble and always be learning, always be asking, always try to grow and do better. When we were mastering our trade shows, we were always looking for the next technologies. We had to stay better than everyone else. Maybe also try to think of yourself less and more of others and your business. Check your motives. Make sure that self-centered fear, the fear of losing what we have, or not getting what we want, isn't your driving force.

One of the great lines about being humble I've heard is that being humble isn't about thinking less of yourself, it's about thinking of yourself less. Think about it. There is nothing worse than being around people who only want to talk about their accomplishments. Remember we do business with those we know, like, and trust so I hope to God I never come off as a know it all. I always want to be learning.

So, what should your motive be? I think that comes down to Simon Sinek's TEDx talk "Start with why." My WHY is that I'm passionate about entrepreneurs' passion. And with that, I fall in love with the clients, their passion, their products, and/or ideas. I love the energy and it just wraps me up. For example, this weekend, a pet project was on mold remediation and asbestos removal. That's not something most people can get passionate about. But the owner of this company is so good and so teachable, and just wonderful. We recently had a horrific storm where a lot of people's pipes burst and there was a need for the product. So, I'm trying to help. That's my why. I'm in a much better place when I'm focused on that, than I am on my own fears. So humble for me isn't thinking less of myself, it's thinking of myself less.

Take a step back and evaluate your business and connect with your WHY. Accept that we are changing. Your WHY might not be being on a podium; it might be creating jobs or helping others. Write out your own statement of purpose that includes your why, so that you can turn to it when you need it from time to time. Use this statement as a tool to know what you stand for.

8. Made a list of all the people we have harmed and mistakes we have made. *Become willing to clean up the mess.*

This is important. Reputation is everything. Clean up your loose ends from previous dealings. I have not done a great job here, in my opinion. I tend to work in a bubble; I'm focused on the bubble and the people in the bubble and when I move on there is some wreckage that I still need to deal with. I will get there when I can. You know who you are, and just know that I'll get there.

This is about amending the past; not our first business; not the first time. Make a list to make amends. Make a list of business mistakes. See where you've gone wrong; see where we are repeating mistakes. We don't have to "take the bait" and fall into the rabbit hole. When you face your past mistakes, it gives you an opportunity to see your weaknesses. See this as a good thing. Because when you point them out to yourself, you are more likely to not make the same mistake again.

There may come a time, or a dozen times, when we are going to start something new. A new business, a new idea, or just do things in a completely different way. Just do it right. Karma is a bitch. Be able to look people in the eye, as you may need help again. Remember if you want advice, ask for money; if you want money, ask for advice, said one of the smarter people I know.

9. Made attempts to correct our past mistakes and/or learn from them. *Clean up the mess.*
Remember you are part of others' mistakes so don't be overzealous here, but do what you need to do to clean up the past and don't let past relationships take the zig out of your zag.

Don't overthink it or judge yourself. Just do it; have a clear conscience and clean up your past. Remember, also, that not everyone is going to love you or even like you. You are doing this for you so you can look everyone in the eye with a clear conscience.

It might be hard to move forward without cleaning up the past. This isn't easy stuff; it takes guts, but we need to know that we are doing this for us. There should be no one we can't look in the eye and have a cup of coffee with.

Put systems in place so you don't make the mistakes again. Clean up from the past.

10. Continued to take personal inventory, when we were wrong promptly admit it. *Staying current with your behavioral goals.*

I have found that nothing can defuse a situation faster than believing and saying that we were wrong. It's not "I am sorry," but "I was wrong," or "It was wrong of me." Notice it doesn't say if we were wrong, but more when we were wrong. There is a difference; no one really cares if you are sorry, but for you and them to know that you were wrong and will try to make things right is completely different. Don't be afraid to admit when you are wrong. We are going to be wrong; we are human.

Maintain what you have. Update your inventory of processes, improve them, and continue to ask for help. When we think we know all the answers we're in trouble. We need to know the questions more than the answers.

Please also get in the habit of looking at your day physically, mentally, spiritually, motivationally, and financially. Only an entrepreneur really knows if he or she is being productive and having a good day or a bad day. We are the only one who knows what our motives and motivators are. Only we know if what we are doing is moving us closer to our goals. Generally, it's not just financial success that stimulates us. Make sure you are staying on the road that takes you to where you want to go.

If nothing else, make sure that you have H.A.L.T. in check. You don't want to become too Hungry, Angry, Lonely, or Tired, or you can get cranky making rash decisions with a sharp tongue. Just keep an eye on it. I don't know about you, but I can forget to eat and then wonder why I am tired and cranky. These are quick, easy fixes.

At On The Bus™, prior to our monthly meetings with our members, we have them fill out their monthly

Bus Pass to track their behavioral goals. We establish behavioral goals every December and June through classes, which you can learn about in the *On The Bus™ WorkBook* in the chapter on behavioral goals.

We can also do spot check inventories when wrestling with decisions. In the old days we would draw a line down a piece of paper and list pros and cons on either side. Today we can do it with S.W.O.T. analysis decisions. We do this with a vertical and horizontal line giving us four equal boxes. We then put Strengths, Weaknesses, Opportunity, and Threats in each quadrant. When I have done this for myself or with the people I coach, we generally have our answers before we are halfway done.

Let's say we are wrestling with whether or not to fire a client, fire an employee, start a new division, raise prices whatever it is, S.W.O.T. it.

Let's use raising prices.

STRENGTHS	WEAKNESSES
We would probably make more and work less. Be more profitable.	We would be less competitive. People could feel ripped off.
OPPORTUNITIES	**THREATS**
Lose some of the smaller high maintenance clients. Finance upcoming projects. Be more prepared for bumpy roads ahead.	Competitors will use it against us. Clients won't be happy...

I think you can see that it's probably a good idea and if handled right could be a win.

Let's do one to consider starting a new division or product offering.

STRENGTHS	WEAKNESSES
Press worthy. Something new to talk to clients about. Good for morale.	Dilute our current resources. Start up costs. Might not work.
OPPORTUNITIES	THREATS
Better margins. First to market, exclusive product.	Sales aren't quick enough. We get embarrassed. Lose a lot of money.

That's a tough one and I'd would say more research and focus groups may be needed.

Here's one for me... Should I write another book?

STRENGTHS	WEAKNESSES
Give us material to franchise with, something to use at future meetings, I'll always be an author and have a call to action when speaking.	Wipes out my energy. Puts me in hermit mode. No one may like it. Could lose a lot of money. Could have spent my time in other ways.
OPPORTUNITIES	**THREATS**
Between the two books and our formula we are now definitely franchisable. People will always know how to improve themselves with the 12 Steps. Could be wonderful.	It's exhausting. Could be humiliating, I may have competition watering down what we do. People may think less of me somehow for my spiritual thoughts and feel a little vulnerable.

Another thing to ask yourself on a regular basis is: Are you working on your business or in it? This isn't just a sound bite. What are you building? Is your business really a hobby you are being paid for? Are you delegating as well as you could be? Here is a graphic that can help you. Stay in the sweet spot where the things you do touch all segments.

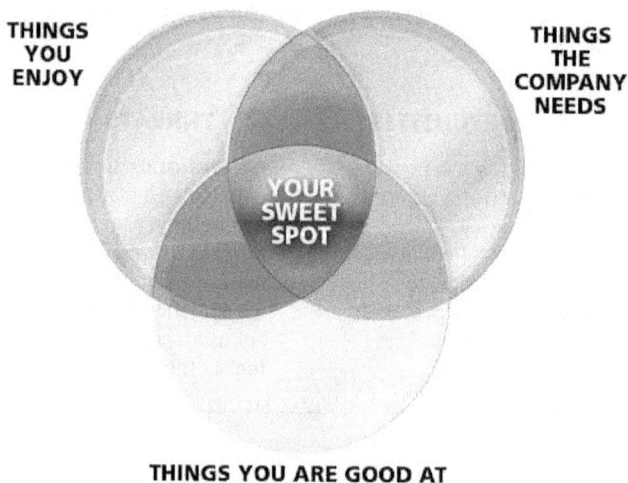

THINGS YOU ARE GOOD AT

11. Sought through prayer, meditation, and managing systems to improve our conscious contact. *Keep growing towards your vision. Keep your vision growing.*

You can't do it alone. I know this goes against the grain, but you can't do it as well alone. The idea of growth isn't to have the same year every year. If you want 10 years of growth, you can't just have the same year 10 times. We need to grow our systems, people, processes, and clients.

Don't keep your head in the sand. Keep going deeper here with your systems, your beliefs, your motives and motivations, your goals, your behavior. Consider all of your goals and your team's goals. Keep growing always; there's no moving backwards, only forward. Some of the most successful people I know are members of multiple mastermind type groups, networking groups, or both. Keep learning, keep improving, keep growing.

It is important to make time to reflect. This can be over a cup of coffee while looking out the window, *not* while checking email on your laptop. It can also come in the form of a walk. Taking time to reflect on our business is a chance to be in the big picture, and to reflect on your WHY (which you created in Step 7). Always take time to smell the roses. Only we really know what success looks like. Enjoy the journey.

Decisions always boil down to what is right, not WHO is right. We know when we need to say something; and when we don't need to say something. WAIT: why am I talking?

We want to improve our business by trusting the process, trusting where we are evolving to. Part of that is our gut, but the greater impact is trusting that your community will guide you in the right direction.

12. Having had success with THESE steps we try to carry THIS messages to other entrepreneurs and to continue practicing these principles in all our affairs. *Give back to others what we've learned in groups like this. Help others!*

This is so important. To be honest, this is where this book began. It's so important to give back in general. For successful entrepreneurs to work with up-and-coming entrepreneurs will be life changing for all.

It will keep the elder grateful and motivated and the youngling full of hope, respect, and gratitude. Please carry the message of entrepreneurship. Give others the courage to make a difference in their lives, themselves, and others. It's so important to carry this message so people know both your success and your failures and that we can grow from our failures.

Whose economy are you working with? I don't consider myself successful by most standards, yet incredibly rich by my own, with the people I get to help and see grow. I can get very emotional over others' success where I know I got the chance to play a role in it. That warms my heart. It fills my pocket; it doesn't fill my bank account, but it's not my motive. I can tell you at the end of every trade show we've done, there's an emotional moment of plain joy that it all worked out, as well as gratitude. Whether we made or lost money isn't the motive.

The lawyer was right about buying the franchise – or was she? Whether it became profitable or not, the knowledge I learned and the confidence I gained are priceless and I think many of us would agree that I am a huge success. At least I think I am; and I still love

Mondays and can't imagine doing anything else and have no plans on stopping.

Know what you are wishing on is gold; have a rudder. Get out of bed and write it down or let the idea die. As for me, I got out of the shower to write this down. This is a way up and out, this is it. If you want to keep what you have, you need to give it away sometimes.

Part of why this book is written was to feature some of the businesses I've helped to pay it forward in being of service to the larger community. Should I have done that? I'm not sure, but I wouldn't know what I know now if I hadn't. That's the value proposition – the why that doesn't get measured in dollars.

It doesn't have to be the On The Bus™ community – it can be any community. Helping the entrepreneur on a path so they can see where mistakes have already been made for them. Embrace mistakes so that we can grow from them, and not make those mistakes again.

Evaluate each business task. There are things that you enjoy, there are things your company needs, and there are things that you're good at. If all three are true, do it yourself. If not, then delegate the task. Find the middle spot; if it touches all three, we do it. If it doesn't, we delegate it. And we should only do the things we really enjoy. For example, we may be good at filing and the company needs it, but we probably don't enjoy it. So, don't do it. Have somebody else do it.

Just a helpful note based on my experience: hiring other entrepreneurs is never a good idea. Once an entrepreneur, always an entrepreneur, and we are a pain in the butt to manage. Also, be careful of teaching your next competitors; keep your people happy and legal them up. What I don't want entrepreneurs to do is to create their own competition. One way we can do that with employees is to create and sign non-disclosures, non-competes, and non-solicits, but the employee thinks they won't hold up. I'm not a lawyer; I don't need to go into all that. Another way to protect yourself is that your employees can be fingers on a hand. The pinky doesn't need to know what the thumb is doing in order to close a fist. For example, if a business owner wants to think in terms of being franchisable, we can get our systems down. The french fry maker doesn't always need to know what the person who is at the cash register is doing. They need to know how to make french fries. They stay in their lanes; they know their roles, but they don't need to know the big picture. The person who does the work doesn't need to know how you get the work. And vice versa. That way, you're not creating your own competition.

Remember where you were when you started. There will always be someone who you will be able to lift up. Be sure to lift them up.

What is On The Bus™? How did it come to be and where are we going?

First let me say that it's been one of the great privileges of my life and a true honor to be a part of the On The Bus™ community. Our members are amazing and I just love being a part of their energy.

Where it started was New Year's Eve 2010, I was listening to the book *Good to Great* on audio. The author Jim Collins writes about having the right people in the right seats on the bus. I was with my girlfriend at the time and she pointed out that it would be a great name for the company. We always like to say: when did you get on the bus? There's also a tongue in cheek reference to the hippie scene in that phrase. Depending on who hears it, they both get it and are both right. Most people reading this identify with Jim Collins' book.

What I was originally doing was teeing up sales opportunities for my clients and creating networking opportunities for them. Then we started teaching them, guiding them on how to get deals and how to close deals. As I got more involved with TAB, On The Bus™ took a backseat. I was coaching a Sandler sales training company, so I didn't feel I could have a competitive brand of my own. That pushed On The Bus™ further back. Once we helped the Sandler franchise get sold, then I was free to revisit On The Bus™. We then started branding the events we were having, like our lunch and learns and networking groups.

To define the experience of On The Bus™, it's a community for business owners that includes monthly Bus meetings that run for four hours. We offer different buses for different stages and sizes of the entrepreneur's journey. Each Bus hosts up to eight owners of similar size. When I define size, it's generally headcount, because that is an identifiable mark of growth as to where they are and what they're thinking. Revenue size doesn't matter as much as the headcount. If they have no employees, if they're strictly going to be a solopreneur, I'll put them on a bus with strictly solopreneurs. They could be doing $5 million a year or $5,000 a year, they're still solopreneurs. They have a similar mindset.

If they've got six or seven employees and they want to have a vision of having 25, that's a different mindset, so we'll have those types of owners together. Or if they're nearing the end, and looking to exit in the next five years, that can be another Bus of how to get them out of their own way.

Between meetings they get one-to-one coaching. The purpose of the coaching is to get them ready for their Bus meeting. I'll meet with the owners several days in advance to make sure they're going to get value from the meeting. So that's where we're going to figure out their challenge or opportunity or what they want to present. It could also be a situation where they have a presentation coming, perhaps to a bank or to an investor or to a large client, and they want to practice it. They can do that there safely, and just role play a little.

There are lots of ways of using their Bus and the community. We offer sales training for all of our members using the *On the Bus™ WorkBook* as a guide. If they want to send their employees, there's a fee. They get a monthly Bus meeting, one-to-one coaching, sales training, and a weekly networking group called V.A.N.G. (Virtual Area Networking Group) on Thursdays. We even met one year on Thanksgiving, it's just that kind of group. Nice people who care about each other. It's a chance to prove your chops, practice, and take a do over if you don't like how your 45 second intro worked. We have a system for all of that as well. Quarterly we have virtual trade shows. We used to have in-person live trade shows a couple of times a year; we went virtual in 2020. Our members now get booths along with their membership. I leave the booths up in between shows that members are able to use as a virtual office. On the Bus™ is an incubator, a community, a think tank, a mastermind group.

On The Bus Preamble

On The Bus™ is a community for Small Business Owners. We share our experience, strength, and hope at weekly meetings with the intent of helping each other grow and achieve success in a safe environment moving our members forward while being kind.

On top of our monthly Bus meetings our members may attend weekly meetings.

- The 1st Friday of the month, Bus Stop, Lunch & Learn, or quarterly Virtual Trade Show.
- The 2nd Tuesday of the month, Sales training using the *On The Bus™ WorkBook* as a guide.
- The 3rd week of the month, A discussion meeting or Social, Social Media.
- The 4th Tuesday of the month, Discuss a chapter from *The Entrepreneur's Big Book™*.
- All meetings are virtual.

You or a guest may come to the first meeting of your choice for free. After that, there is a fee, this does not include Bus numbered meetings, for those you must be vetted and an accepted member.

The format of this meeting is as follows:

Discussion Meeting Format

We start with 45-second introductions of everyone in the room. The chairperson picks a leader to tell their entrepreneurial story in a general way and wrap it up with a topic that we will discuss. The topic may be one that they struggle with or feel that they are an expert on. We will discuss the topic giving each a chance to share for 2-5 minutes depending on the number of people. The leader speaks for about 12 minutes. Ready, all aboard, let's go.

Sales Training Format

We start every meeting with 45-second introductions. We then have an open forum to discuss sales challenges and get feedback from the group. Then we have a topic discussion from one of the chapters, listening to it on Audible.

Bus Stop Format

We start with 45-second introductions of everyone in the room. The chairperson introduces the speaker and pays for the room. Presenter pays for lunch. Presenter speaks for roughly an hour on a topic they are an expert on, infomercial, not a sales opportunity.

Where we are going...

Now that this book is done, and all our formats are protected with the USPTO, we are ready to franchise and welcome those conversations. We have a formula that is really exciting, works really well and can work anywhere.

ESSAYS BY ON THE BUS™ COMMUNITY ENTREPRENEURS

What follows is my favorite part of the book and will hopefully be yours. I find these stories to be motivating and inspiring. I thank all of you who have contributed. One of the intentions of this book is that it be used for group discussions in our On The Bus™ meetings as topics. The short essays in the middle of the book are personal stories of entrepreneurs sharing what life and business used to be like, what changes and pivots they made when joining a group like On The Bus™, and what life and business are like now. The intent is not to say how great On The Bus™ or Chris Lipper are, although it's nice to hear and humbling to know the difference we've made. The intent is more to share entrepreneurs' stories, mistakes and solutions in a general way. Please try to identify with the writers' feelings and intentions rather than comparing their blow-by-blow accounts. As the saying goes, it doesn't matter if you came from Yale or jail, Park Avenue or a park bench – the feelings are all the same. Entrepreneurs share passion, it is what makes us tick, share yours with your group.

Lois Manzella Marchitto
Owner, Fitness Knocking

"My coach, Chris, says good is the enemy of great. He taught me so much about being in business, but he also taught me to be ok being uncomfortable."

I am unsure specifically where my drive for entrepreneurship began. I do know I always wanted to have my own money. I was always a saver and thinking about how to get what I want. I grew up in suburbia in Jefferson Township in Morris County, New Jersey, in a beautiful, contemporary home. My father was an immigrant from Sicily who came to the United States as a boy. He was an entrepreneur and the sole provider, owning a hair salon since he was a young adult. I worked at my parents' hair salon when I was old enough to sweep the floor and stock shelves and throughout middle and high school. I got my second job when I was 13, teaching three dance classes a week. Then when I turned 16 I became a dance teacher, teaching my own classes. I had a jazz and ballet class for five year-olds and a hip-hop class for my peers, who were 12-17 year-olds. I loved seeing the image of the 15 students learning from me. I loved planning, being in charge, and being the leader. I was never afraid of work.

Fast forward to after high school when one day, while working out at the gym, the owner started talking to me and encouraged me to get a personal training certificate. She said I had a great eye for detail and technique. There was a part of me that wanted my own business. I just didn't know what. The thing I didn't love about my parents' business was that my parents owned their job or technically their business owned them. They couldn't have real vacations (over four days) because taking time off meant not getting paid.

While I was still in college, I made my first attempt at business. A friend, who was another personal trainer and fellow foodie, thought we would make it rich making and selling "healthy" baked goods. We set up an entity, got checks, made a business plan, opened a bank account and bought business cards. Our business was called "L's Edibles." We worked out of a bagel store at night and would lay out all of our ingredients, set up our mixers, and get to work making healthy muffins, cookies, and pancakes. We truly thought the world needed us. Our friendship grew initially as we were excited, but then we slowly realized we knew how to bake, but that was about it. We sold our items at the bagel place and at the gym we worked at, but we only made enough to pay our expenses. Then Y2K happened. [When moving from 1999 to 2000 created technical problems for many.] My partner needed a real job and I tried to work it by myself, but quickly realized business was hard, dealing with business partners was hard, selling was hard, and just because I built it doesn't mean they will come. Our little company L's Edibles was here and gone in a year.

I chose the safe route and got a job as a high school dance teacher and a health teacher. I wanted more, needed more, and was willing to burn all of my ships to make it happen. In what felt like one second, I was buying an existing business, quitting my jobs, and jumping off a cliff into the unknown. Three years later, I now own my company and my time; I am much happier and can help you lovely people get more of what you want. I hope to give you some tools to take away and some tips that have helped me become successful.

I started working with Chris after I had another business coach. I had just started my company about seven months prior to meeting Chris. In retrospect, it was a pretty risky, ballsy type of move. I came from public education. I was a high school teacher. Given that background of really knowing my craft, but not understanding the business side, was quite the education. I didn't know what I was doing when I took over someone else's business. I paid a lot of money for it. I had a business coach, who was very nice. And I'm grateful to him, because he was the one who sent me to this LinkedIn® training where I met Patty Singer. She was trying to teach me about LinkedIn®; my head was spinning, because I'm not really good with social media – or technology for that matter. She said, "why don't you try networking?" And I replied, "What's that?" I'd never heard of networking. She introduced me to Chris and gave me some really good advice. She said, "you need to hire a business coach and work with a team of people who can give you feedback, and who can provide you with support that you need in order to grow your business." I signed on with Chris and On The Bus™ as my business coach and worked with him for a really long time. And I'm very grateful that I did so.

What was my business life like before that? I was scared and unclear of what the future would hold for me, if I had to sum it up in a couple of words. I learned a lot. What Chris did was ask the right questions to guide me – just like you can guide a sales process through questions, just like you can guide your spouse through questions and your kids through questions. He really taught me to be a master craftsperson in the art of questioning, and gave me a lot of support and the guidance I needed to ask the right questions to get the answers that my clients needed to move forward. One of the things he taught me right from the start was how to network and how to build relationships and build a tribe of people who support and help my business thrive. I can't say enough nice things about that.

A lot of things changed after I started working with Chris. I got confident in my abilities to grow my brand and understand what branding was and understand the marketing side and the sales process and hiring and firing. There are so many things that I didn't know; the list could probably go on for pages. I was an excellent technician. When I met Chris and joined On The Bus™, I definitely knew my craft. What I didn't know was what I didn't know. He helped to give me the ideas of what I didn't know. I thought it was like the movie *Field of Dreams*®: "If you build it, they'll come."

Thinking about the mistakes I made and learned from that could benefit other business owners, there were so many. I think the biggest one is not being patient. That was my biggest challenge and that still rears its ugly head once in a while – being impatient when it comes to myself and my learning process. This wasn't my first attempt at business ownership. I think one of my biggest mistakes, besides not being patient, was not having a real clear understanding of how long things take, and how much money you need to have – such as products in storage – to get your business up and running. In addition to the operation expenses, you know, having the means to pay for a service like On The Bus™. It's costly to work with any kind of business coach or work with a marketing person. There are so many hats; I didn't know all of the hats that were involved when I jumped in, but I didn't have a backup plan, so I just had to swim. My family was counting on me. In the beginning I just said, "Alright, it's going to be do or die. I'm just going to keep at it. I'm just going to keep working hard." I think it is a big mistake a lot of business owners make – you want instant gratification, instant results. I had to pedal back and say, "Wait a second. Everything takes time. I have to be patient. I have to be understanding. I have to do the process. I have to create the system."

Another major mistake is that I bought someone else's business. It was a hell of a learning mistake for me. I think if I had met Chris and was On The Bus™ a year before I was thinking about buying this business and was consulting with him, I think I would have just started my own business and not bought someone else's. Everything had to be reinvented anyway. I'm grateful that I had a support system to be able to invent and create on my own. I pretty much reinvented the company anyway. Changing the name of my company was a mistake. It meant changing the website to a new domain. *That* was a big mistake – a hard mistake to figure out because I lost all my analytics; I lost all the data. I hadn't considered the effect changing the domain would have. But that was before I got On The Bus™.

When it comes to sales and my business, I was giving up too soon. That's a mistake. That one comes up every once in a while, where I just give up and do not follow up. Just give up and not wait for the "No." I don't like hearing the word no, it is just hard to hear it. But those are valuable lessons. Because if you start with no, then okay, you don't need us. Okay, great. Who do you know who might need us? Even being okay with being told no and hearing it as they are not saying no to you necessarily. It's that they're saying no to themselves, or they're saying no to the process. Now when people say no, I ask them, "no forever, or no for right now?" I've learned that throw yourself under the bus phrase. My biggest fear is that you're never going to call, or my biggest fear is I was afraid to ask because I didn't want to come off salesy, or that I was all about money, or that people didn't like me. But now I know. I don't get stumped by that stuff anymore.

Now my network is pretty big. Networking is the primary way to grow my business. Chris said it would be; I just didn't realize how long it would take. I wasn't patient. It takes a while. I don't have a while. I have to pay my bills now, so I can eat now. Being impatient, that was my biggest hurdle. My biggest mistake. Being patient with the process – and if it doesn't work, being okay saying I messed up the way things are done, throw it out, and start over. The caveat is being polite and patiently waiting. And then kind of timing out when you follow up. When it comes to that big NO, it's like, okay, they're not saying no to me personally, but No to the process. It's purely financial; if people don't have a budget, it's a no brainer.

I get such crazy excuses from people about why they're not continuing. Sometimes it's an easy fix. For example, I had a client who was working with one of our trainers, and the trainer was giving her what she asked for. But sometimes what a client asks for, and what they need are two different things.

I have great success stories with clients who ultimately wouldn't have worked with me had I not used the skills I learned through working with Chris. Chris isn't magic. Chris asks the right questions and can guide you in ways that make you uncomfortable.

THE RADIATOR GUY
A CONVERSATION WITH THE RADIATOR GUY

Where He Came From, Where He Went, and Where He Ended Up...

My parents are originally from Puerto Rico. They immigrated during the 1950s as children. My dad has had a business here, a factory, since 1991. It was a small factory. He was in his 70s and he was just using it to entertain himself. And then I bought into the company and realized after eight months that I wasn't the corporate type. I'm here and we made the move here and I don't regret it in the least. It's been a really good thing.

My company is growing pretty fast, and my staff has major rules. One of the rules is to never give me an original document of any sort because they know I'll lose it.

I was born and raised in Jersey City, New Jersey. My dad's a Vietnam veteran, and after he came back from Vietnam, he was looking for sort of a specialty. He was an aircraft mechanic and he fell into the radiator business. So, I grew up in that. We had a small shop in North Bergen, New Jersey, right on the border of Jersey City. I helped out in my spare time – you know, solder, clean up, and drive, basically do whatever was needed. Then I went to Rutgers University in New Brunswick. After I graduated from Rutgers, I did internships in finance. I was a trading assistant for a municipal bond trader, worked on Wall Street, worked in Jersey near Newport, and did that for a while. I just realized it wasn't for me, and I didn't see a future in it. I didn't really like it. I didn't like throwing on a suit and having to go into the subway.

Subsequently, I met this girl, and she was going to be traveling through Southeast Asia. I had never heard of such a thing, but decided to give it a try! I gave my boss 30 days' notice, and I bought a ticket to Vietnam – no reservations, no nothing. I didn't know the language or anything about the place, really. I went to Vietnam and wanted to see where my dad was and kind of understand his history a little bit better. That was awesome, and I did that for a month. I returned to the states, but longed to return. I had learned how to ride a motorcycle in Vietnam; when I came back to the states I bought one and a few months later went back to Cambodia. I met this kid online and he was looking for somebody to ride around with. We proceeded to ride our motorcycles for the next three months through Cambodia, Thailand, and Laos. I left just before the tsunami of 2004 and went home. I didn't really have any plans at that point. My dad's manager at the time needed some help. I joined the family business, never left, and then started seeing the possibilities.

I had a lot of confidence after taking that trip through Southeast Asia as I began to understand what was possible. It just gave me a lot of self-confidence to be able to do something that I thought not a lot of people had the guts to do, so I proceeded to just make a lot of changes and identify market opportunities and get into different things. It went very well. My father isn't super sophisticated with digging into financial statements. He would constantly ask questions like: why is your inventory going up dramatically? I was reinvesting all the profits in inventory so that I could sell more. I made a lot of connections in the industry.

The Radiator Guy's Business Experiences

In 2010, I bought the company from my father. He knew I really wanted to take it to another level. I acquired the company from him and started doing my own thing. I proceeded to continue growing the company. I made some major connections and I got into something called DPF (Diesel Particulate Filter) cleaning. All the new trucks from 2008 and up had filters that needed to be serviced. In 2009, I bought the machine to service them, and then proceeded to wait a year for my first one to come in. All my friends were making fun of me asking me how my pizza oven was doing. Lo and behold, as things developed, we became DPF's premier cleaner in New Jersey. Then, in 2013, I made a very strategic alliance with a couple other shops; we formed sort of an informal buying group and we were able to purchase directly from the premier distributor in China. Everybody wanted it; we were able to get it. That turbo boosted my business. Then a Fortune 500 company came sniffing around. I talked to the other companies from our buying group, and I said we're on top now, we might want to consider selling. Those guys were 20 years older than me, so they were receptive to it because they were looking for an exit strategy. I didn't know if I could maintain that kind of profitability for much longer without having to make massive investments. We did the deal, and I sold out in November of 2016. I stayed with that company until August of 2017.

At the end of August I bought 50% of the shares of a company in Puerto Rico. In September of 2017 Hurricane Maria hit – Puerto Rico's biggest hurricane in 100 years. I was in New Jersey. For a week, we didn't even know if there was a company; there was no communication. Finally, after about a week, somebody uploaded something to Facebook. It was a video going through the small town where we have the company, and they pan in on the factory. Not only is it open, but there's a line of people outside because there's no electrical grid and we're the only ones on the whole island that can make a radiator for generators. All these generators that have deferred maintenance for 20 years are breaking left and right. We just had this turbo boost. Sometimes it's better to be lucky than good. I used to argue with my father if you're the only factory, why not just do just in time inventory; why carry all this raw material? He always just said, you're on an island, things happen, you never know. And then things happened. We went through a year's worth of inventory in three months. That boom lasted a year and a half, so we were able to build the bases that we never had, since I was here. We were able to get product knowledge that no one in the world had. That gave the company a huge base that we continue to build upon, that we continue to pivot off of, and we're dramatically expanding the company.

Then COVID hits. We had 50 employees. I talked to my father. During Hurricane Maria, everybody was here for us. I said, "Now it is *our* time to give." We didn't know there was going to be PPP business relief, so we paid everybody from day one. They gave us permission to open up, because we're an essential service as nobody else can make what we make. We had 30% of the workforce working, and those 30% are in double pay. Everybody else stayed home and got that payment. When it was time to come back, all the companies that laid off their workers, their workers didn't come back, because they were making more money, but we've had this stable workforce. The supply chain aspect that was a result of the pandemic has been a benefit for us. Because we're a niche factory, we're not going to make 100 of anything;

we're going to make one of something that weighs 1,000 pounds, and then we'll make one of something that weighs 40 pounds, and then the line just keeps changing. We're like a custom shop. All across the world, people who were used to getting product with a lead time of three or four weeks, were now waiting 16 to 18 weeks. It's been opening up huge doors, especially considering we'd never exported anything before. Now my goal is to get to 50% in exports within two to three years. I think we're probably going to do that in less than a year.

I did make some changes after getting On The Bus™ and working with Chris. Mostly, I was very closed. I didn't like to tell anybody about my business. I had a couple of confidants in my industry, but to have a group with whom I was able to share my business with was critical at that point in my career, especially considering I was young, in my early 30s. I had a pretty successful business. I'm a lot different; I've evolved. But even with that group, I never shared really detailed numbers. I was always concerned that someone was going to come in and steal my business or something. Knowing what I know, now, I realized there's so many barriers to entry to certain types of businesses, especially one like mine. It was really good to have a sounding board of people. Everybody now experiences most of the time the same stuff – employees, challenges with partners, challenges with clients, how do you handle growth? So, at that point, it was really critical for me and informative to have to see a bunch of people that didn't have a vested interest; they weren't an accountant, somebody you're paying. They just want to hear because you're part of this group, and they're going to give you their objective opinion, without someone thinking, what's their ulterior motive?

Here's what happened as a result – what changed in my business life as a result of becoming involved with On The Bus™. I'll give you a perfect example. I didn't have a lot of experience, and I'm growing this business. I remember I was hemming and hawing on whether I was going to hire this counter guy that was critical. And I remember one of my On The Bus™ members saying, "You've been talking about this for four or five months; just do it. What's the worst thing?" That gave me that push that I needed. Sometimes I'm either a ready, fire, aim guy and boom, let's go. That's usually for me with the stuff I understand, like a machine. Let's buy it and we'll figure it out when it gets here, whether we have the electrical capacity to run it or whatever. But human resources, sort of softer problems like that, the Bus was able to give me these pushes. It was that other sort of softer aspects of running a business; you have someone who says, "shit, or get off the pot." "Why are you doing this?" "You need this." And I have seen that happen on many occasions in our meetings, and it helped me make decisions that I had to make – and I could see other businessmen, and how they did things, and learn what to do – and also certain times learn what not to do. But I encourage anyone to get involved in a group like On The Bus™, or a business peer group, because you don't know it all. If you think you know it all, that's probably a bad sign. Even just listening to different ideas and spitballing stuff is amazingly valuable.

I run my company very differently. Now, I've delegated a lot. The company I had before was kind of like my own one-man show. I kept it very, very close to the vest, a lot of sensitive information. Now I do things differently. I've evolved as a businessperson; I'm always learning. Right now, I'm learning how to make a critical hire. I've never had to hire a high-level employee. I have my own sort of management group, then I have guys in the industry who I just bounce stuff off of. You're talking stuff that's really granular to the industry. Especially when you're starting out, you need to have some people to guide you. It's tremendously valuable. As I look back now, and you talk about the right people, and delegate to elevate, and measure yourself by how little you're needed in the business. I first heard that at an On The Bus™ meeting by a man named Jeff Barry, who had a generator maintenance company. A lot of times if you're in your own little business, and you're working in your business versus on your business, you've got to hear that from people, because a lot of times you read a book and it just sounds like just some mumbo jumbo pop science kind of stuff. But when you see people actually implement, and then you see the results, and you go to their business, and you see the vibe of the business and how they're not stressed out. When I first started in On The Bus™, my phone would be ringing constantly, and I used to think that was cool. I used to think that to be a businessman is to be on the phone constantly, that you've got things going on. I didn't have anybody to tell me no. Now, being a good businessman means you have people in place to handle that. The only calls you're taking are on your terms or emergencies.

Thinking about some of the mistakes that I made that other people could learn from – as you grow, open up; be open. Having an open book business and having people feel part of it is amazingly powerful. Having people all pushing in the same direction, rather than you trying to carry everything is amazingly powerful. Freedom costs money. Getting good people who can handle stuff is a quality-of-life thing. I can go on and on about mistakes on selling your business. Probably the biggest mistake is that I was so closed; I wasn't reaching out. When you're selling a business, especially to a very large company, and you're a small company, they've bought hundreds of businesses before, and you've never sold one – one that you have an emotional attachment to. You are at a major disadvantage. You need to find someone who can help you through that. Chances are your accountant is not the best person to help you in the sale. Chances are your lawyer, who's helped you close on some properties, and maybe he's done some small contract work, is not the guy to help you. The problem is that most of the time those people think you're going to sell, and they may be unwilling or unable to recommend the proper people to do it.

A lot of these mistakes I made, though, are unknowns. You don't know what you don't know, until you're on the other side of the situation. I know the people now to contact only because I've gotten to this level, and I have access to them, but before that I didn't. You don't know who to trust. I didn't like to broadcast a lot of what we were doing and whatnot. I did well in the sale, but I didn't do as well as I perhaps could have. And from a planning standpoint, and from a tax efficiency standpoint, even from a negotiation standpoint, when you're selling your business, and you're dealing with a large company, you shouldn't be negotiating that yourself because to the guys on the other side of the table, you're just another company. For you, it's an emotional thing and they know how to pull all those strings and push those buttons and how to sort of get you to do what's in their best interest and not in your best interest. So now in my industry, I'm the guy to talk to if you're looking to sell your business. I'm happy to do so. I feel like I've been put in a position where I have some knowledge that perhaps other people don't have yet and I'm happy to share that.

In a number of ways, my life changed – for the better, since I made these moves. I grew up and I had never moved out of an eight-mile radius of Jersey City. I've traveled quite a bit, but I've never lived elsewhere with the exception of New Brunswick in college. When I moved to Puerto Rico, it was a difficult transition for me, for many reasons. People don't realize the psychological impact of selling your business. I sold that business and basically what that means is you take something you put your heart and soul into that you care about a lot, and you basically monetize it into a series of zeros and numbers. You realize the initial sort of euphoria of having a significant amount of money materialize. You then realize that that's all it is, a bunch of numbers. You give them the business and they give you money and now it's theirs. Now you have to reconcile that with the emotional part of it. You have employees who have been with you for years; now you're watching them have to fill out applications so they could get hired by the other company. Then they're going to start complaining about stuff. You soon quickly realize that, whereas a week ago you had the power to solve any issues that your employees might have, now, you don't have that power and it is frustrating. I left that company because it just wasn't a fit for me; I'm not a corporate guy. Big companies take a long time to do things and that's not for me.

Then when it came to Puerto Rico, having lived in a small area of Hudson County all my life, where you know the pizza guy, you know all the restaurants, and everybody knows your name. It's like the TV show *Cheers®*. Then you are in a place where you're not exactly a foreigner, or you're not exactly what they call a mainlander, but you're not a local, either; you're in the middle. I found it very isolating. I made the biggest mistake in my life. We bought a house to remodel after Hurricane Maria and it took forever. It was just a nightmare. We moved four times in a year and a half. We finally settled in where we're living now and then everything was cool. My advice is, if you sell your company, don't make a lot of big changes right away. Do it slowly, so you can basically adjust to a new life. Otherwise, life here is great. I love it. The weather's awesome. People are great. I'm very accustomed to living here. Somehow, some way, I kind of always knew that I would end up here.

I get a real joy out of developing the company. There's not a lot of opportunity for people to get good paying jobs. For me, it's kind of like a mission to provide a good quality work environment where they can actually raise a family. I'm the only one of my whole family that's come back. It makes it kind of a mission for me; I don't do it for the money. Yeah, this company is successful, but it's not about that anymore. It's about how many points can we put on the board? How many good bonuses can we give out a year? Can we increase the bonuses? Can we increase the wages that people get and still be successful? When I see my employees get a brand-new car and send their kid to private school, now I feel I've been given the opportunity to be able to do that, and to be able to affect change. We affect 50 employees directly, and indirectly, their families.

I'm not flashy by nature, I don't drive fancy cars or anything like that; my employees know that. What I like to buy – our toys are usually machines that I have no idea how to run; I don't even know how to turn them on. But I like seeing them use it. And I like seeing them work safely. When I see a product 100% made here in Puerto Rico going to Iowa or Baltimore or Kentucky; we sent a radiator to England the other day. That gives me a rush.

We focus on hard to find obsolete or long lead time items – things that they can't find. I'm not looking to compete with China or the Dominican Republic or Mexico. I'm looking for niche opportunities. I say there's riches in the niches.

I realized I made the right move in Puerto Rico, where one day I took my kayak to the local river here. It was just awesome. I realized it's January. I just couldn't be doing this in Jersey. I'm so happy and so grateful. Every day I take bike rides, and I'm just very fortunate that I'm here and that I have the job I have.

Dan Keller
CEO, George Keller & Sons Roofing
A View From the Rooftop

My father actually started the company in 1980. I was two years old at the time when he started. I think I kind of started working for him on weekends, when I was probably in third or fourth grade cleaning up. I worked for him all the way through high school and college on the weekends. That was good, because it was fun money, gas money, and beer money at the time. When I was working for him, I was the last person who would have ever thought that I would still be in this business. I hated the job because it took me away from my friends. It was hard work, which I hated too. When I was really young, I walked off the job site; I was even asleep on the job site. My brothers and sisters would always say, "don't even bring him because he's more of a liability than anything."

When I graduated college and got my Bachelor of Science in Computer Information Systems, I said to my father, "Alright, I'm going to stop working for you on the weekends. I'm going to go get a real job, is what I call it." The first six months out of college, I worked for a small company. I just worked for a local company doing bookkeeping for them. And it was just really a placeholder for me to find a real job. I ended up with Chubb insurance, in their IT department, using my degree, which really was what I wanted to do. Around my second anniversary there, I had my annual review, and I remember my boss telling me, "You've been here two years, you're highly ranked, which is great, but you're never going to move up in corporate America." And I said, "What do you mean?" He replied, "You work really hard, but you don't kiss enough." I said, "What do you mean?!" "You put your head down and you get to work, which is great, because we love the fact that you're very productive, but nobody sees you. The higher-ups don't see you. You need to go out and talk with them and bullshit with them and play the game." I tried it.

About a year later, my father called me and he said, "Hey, we're looking to continue to grow. Would you be willing to leave Chubb and come work for me?" He said, "I'll make you a salesman and pay commission." I said, "When you're ready, I'm ready." A year after that conversation with my boss, I'm tired of bull; I'm tired of kissing people's ass. My five-year anniversary is when I left Chubb. I waited until I was actually fully vested with my 401k.

To backtrack a little bit, when I graduated college, my father combined with my oldest brother and became partners. He invested some money into the business, so they become partners and that's when the company really started to grow. By the time I got there, it was really a full-fledged make a living company. In the spring of 2006, I came aboard. By 2009, I was selling so much that I asked to be a part owner in the business. I kind of gave my brother and my father an ultimatum. I said, "Listen, I'm selling for you guys; I'm making you guys a lot of money. You're not paying me what I need. Either I'm leaving, or you make me a partner." We negotiated and I actually bought my father's shares of the company, so my brother Mike and I were partners for six years. In the spring of 2015, my brother decided he wanted to leave the company and go try something else completely outside of construction. I bought him out. Since 2015, I've been the owner of the company along with my wife.

With all those family dynamics, it did not always go smoothly. My sister came on board as a secretary.

When I bought my father out, he actually became an employee. He didn't retire. He just said, "I don't want to be an owner anymore. And you want to be, so buy my shares out and I'll become an employee." We still had a lot of family members involved. When I bought my brother out in 2015, it wasn't contentious until after the sale. I realized that he was doing things that he shouldn't have been and it screwed me a bit because I was now the owner of the company and I had to pay a whole lot of back taxes. It did hurt the family a little bit, but it was all mended eventually.

When did I realize I needed some outside help? Almost right away. I needed help the day after I bought the business. Of course, I didn't realize it then. So, it was probably in the fall of 2017 that I met Chris at a chamber event and talked to him. Coincidentally, the next day I had a one to one with somebody else that I knew. He said to me, "Chris has helped me tremendously. I highly recommend you talk to him. He'll help you." You won't realize that you need help until you actually commit to it. That actually sold me on it. It was even before I met with Chris; the referral sold me. Then Chris and I sat down, and we went through what it would take. I thought, Oh, shit, how am I going to afford that? Then he said, "And by the way, it's also a four-hour commitment per meeting per month." I said to him, "There's no way I'm going to be able to do that. I am going to get interrupted 8 million times during this meeting." So, I committed to it. I remember my very first meeting. One of the members was actually in the process of selling his business. When I explained all about myself and the problems I was having, he said to me, "Dan, you were me. I was you." I was trying to do everything. I'm not good enough at everything I was trying to do and not trusting anybody to do it better. I feel like I was drowning. He goes, "I was literally you three years ago, and opened my eyes." I said, all right. It's not just me who has these problems. It's other people, too. He said, "Talk with us; we'll get you to where you need to be."

Besides what I alluded to with my brother, other things were overwhelming me in taking on the business. I was trying to be a salesman; I was trying to be an operations manager. I was trying to be the HR department. I had a bookkeeper on staff, so I wasn't trying to be the bookkeeper, but I also didn't understand what the bookkeeping was all about. I was literally trying to be every aspect of the business. I was trying to be the person in charge, failing miserably.

I knew I needed to make changes. The first thing I did is started trusting people because that's what the On The Bus™ group told me – and letting go of the ownership of what you're trying to hand off to somebody. I had to trust that my sister could do some HR or my top project manager could actually run the operations department; trust the sales group that I don't have to go out and sell every job. The first big thing was establishing trust with my existing employees. The second thing was coming up with better processes and procedures that we could put in place that would allow my employees to succeed with the responsibilities I was giving them. We didn't really have anything written down; we kind of winged it. We started putting those processes on paper. It was written down somewhere that we all agree that this is how we should do this task. It was something that everyone could follow. If something wasn't followed, something broke down, at least we knew we could find out where that breakdown was.

After doing that, we started becoming profitable again. The first couple of years that I owned the business, we were not profitable at all. I remember talking to my accountant saying, "Well, what the hell am I going to do?" He goes, "I don't know, but you have to figure it out." I remember thinking, I can't raise my rates; there's no way we're going to get more business, if we raise our rates. I can't afford to pay people and we got into some pretty good debt. I was in a Bus meeting complaining about how I can't afford this, and I can't afford that and this one wants a raise, but I can't afford it. And the other one wants us to add more employees, and I can't afford it. And I remember Chris saying to me, "Hey, how do you take your payments? What's your payment terms?" We do 50% down and then 50% at the end of the job. He goes, "Well, you're putting too much money at the end of the job; why don't you switch it and do a third, a third, a third?" And I said to him, "No way. It's never going to work. We've always done it this way." He was cool. "All right, no problem." The following month, I'm complaining about the same thing. He goes, "Dan, why don't you do what we talked about, doing a third, a third, a third?" I said, "Okay, fine, I'll shut you up. I'll do it." It made a huge difference. Breaking up the payments, all of a sudden, the cash flow in my business was so much better. Even though we still weren't profitable yet, cash flow was better. Then we started becoming more profitable. My personal life and my stress level came down because I wasn't trying to do everything. I trusted everybody that they would do what they're supposed to do. It truly made a world of difference for me and the business.

My advice to other entrepreneurs, as far as getting a mentor or a coach involved? I love it, because I talk to this group and Chris about things that I don't talk to anybody else about, even my wife. A lot of the stuff we talk about is sensitive information and most times not good information. That would stress out my wife, even though she's a partner; she'd worry too much. I don't want to talk to existing employees about it because it's none of their damn business and sometimes it's about them. For an entrepreneur, the group is just a way to talk to your peers about things you cannot talk to anybody else about. You need to talk to somebody because trying to make the decision on your own and solve a problem on your own is sometimes too much. You need to know what options are out there. When I bring a problem to the group, it's a problem where I'm looking for multiple angles; I'm looking for different solutions to the one problem. This is what we've done when we've encountered this. The best part about it is if I get two or three different options, I can pick and choose what I think would be best for the company.

Besides the failure to delegate or let go in the beginning, mistakes I learned from that could benefit other business owners were: my biggest mistake was definitely trying to do too much. Secondly, is learning to separate your business and your personal life. Make sure that you still have a personal life, along with the business. Make sure that your personal relationships are still healthy, along with your business relationships. That is something that is huge. I finally started realizing that it made a big difference for me and my stress level. I learned to say no; you can't say yes to everybody. When I finally learned to say no, with the help of the group, is when my business started being better and again, more profitable. When I started saying no, my business grew and my confidence grew as well.

PETER BORBAS
BORBAS SURVEYING & MAPPING, LLC

Ever since I was a kid, I've kind of been an entrepreneur – cutting lawns, blowing snow, paper routes, things like that. I've always worked, and I like the idea of working and making a dollar. I had that in me to begin with. During college, I found out about surveying; I had a minor in it. One thing led to another, and I ended up becoming a surveyor and actually ended up being Chair of the American Congress of Surveying and Mapping. When I started college I had no idea what a surveyor did. I worked for about eight years for a couple of different firms after college. I worked six hours, six days a week. I wanted Wednesdays off to ski so that I didn't have to ski on weekends. With their big company bureaucracy, they couldn't figure out how to just let me work five days a week and let me have Wednesdays off, so I quit.

I had an ex-employer who helped set me up in business and I started skiing every Wednesday and started a company. We predominantly did residential work, but I had a liking towards the environmental end of things. It's one of the reasons I went to college to begin with and ended up building a rapport with a number of large and small environmental engineering companies. Eventually, there was a lot more money in that work than there was in residential, and I developed a reputation in that area. That's prior to meeting Chris and getting on the Bus with him. I remember my first meeting, and have it in writing, that my purpose for being there, to my Bus members, was that I wanted to ski on better snow more often. I wanted them to tell me how to run my business so that I could do that.

We had challenges prior to that. Cash flow was my biggest problem. That was always challenging as we were moving into the area of working for corporate America, like the big 500, as opposed to residential property owners. It was different. There were other things that had to be addressed. An interesting thing was that I had always thought that when I retire from my business, that I would just give the business off to my second in command.

My Bus members and Chris helped me to understand that there was value in the business that I had built;

the reputation that we had was worth a lot of money, right there. That actually a company could be sold, or it could be leveraged; I just never thought about that. That was a neat thing, and I created a more sustainable business. There was a lot of coaching there about what a sustainable business looks like. That's it; the lightbulb went off. I can remember when folks were talking about franchising. What does a franchise look like, and that if we put all the tools in place, to be able to franchise – not that I wanted to franchise the business, but if we had the tools in place to franchise the business, one would think that we could grow the value of the business. If it were ever to be sold and become a lot more attractive, putting the things in place, protecting me legally. That was a huge one. It was cutting out a lot of risk. Having things like I never had before, like an employee manual. I had other business owners who were sharing their ideas on employee handbooks, etc. There were things such as standard operating procedures. What are your checklists? How do you do these things consistently, and your quality checks? All these kinds of franchise things got put into place, and there's a standard to operate in business. This is how we did things.

Another thing folks helped me to understand is that if I just said no to some of the business that I didn't want, then there'll be more time to grow it to where I wanted to be, which would give me more time. The problem nowadays is we've got such a reputation that everybody wants us, so I spend my time just telling people No, or just turning out a lot of proposals, getting the work and trying to figure out how to get it done. One thing we did is when phone calls would come in or emails would come in my office manager was able to vet those things. She says, "This is something that we're not interested in and that's not what we do; it's not our forte." She's got a list of other surveyors that she refers people to.

As I said, cash flow is a huge problem. I learned to tighten up my contracts. I learned that I didn't have to be pushed around by Big Five Fortune 500 companies; I could stand up to them and say, "No, I'm not signing the subcontractor agreement. Those aren't my terms. These are my terms. These are my payment terms, etc., and these are my insurance limits. If you want us, then you'll change your terms." Surprisingly enough, I found out there are a number of folks who would actually do that. When they said they could never pay retainers, well, I'm sorry, we're not working for you. That helped the cash flow mentally. I'm very, very happy to say that we've got a very nice cushion in case we hit another recession or a downturn in the market. I'm very comfortable about the way things are financially.

Interestingly enough, over the last few years, we've been recognized by a number of national firms larger than us that have approached me to buy my company. That is very, very flattering. If I didn't have the wonderful situation that I have, and the wonderful people that I'm working with, I might entertain that. I understand that some company that wants to buy another surveying company today is buying them because they cannot find people to work. There are very few surveyors out there; there are so few people who go into school for this, so the way they get people is they buy up other companies. It's almost like buying slaves in a way. I'm not going to do that to the people I work with; they have so much invested in it. I think they expect that they can be there for life and they're going to get treated really well and they're paid well. It's just a great atmosphere; you can give bonuses.

My plan is to sell the business to my current second in command who has been there for 12 years and is younger than I am. He'd like to have me stay on. If I were to sell my company to some entity, I'd typically have to stay on for three to five years, they'd take all the money, and I'd just be an employee.

I like to work and retirement for me is something similar to what I've been doing for the last 36 years. Going canoeing, fishing, skiing, traveling vacations with my wife, and having great relationships with my clients and other folks who we meet and work with. I really like my life. I like what we do. I'm getting tired of some of the headachy kind of things and whatnot. Retirement for me is maybe when there's some kind of problem that I don't have to get the phone call – somebody else in the company gets the phone call, and that I can spend my time mentoring the younger folks in the company, and not just the younger folks, but even the second in command. I mean, I've got 45 years of great experience that I want to share with folks. I think there's a lot of value in that. I'm having fun doing what I'm doing. I'll continue to do it and make a decent buck.

So, I figured out how to get all that skiing in. The solution is to have not just the systems that are in place but the people in place – the right people; the right people to do the jobs that our clients need to have done. Everybody's different in their abilities and their knowledge. Don't expect them to do something that they're not good at. As Chris would say, having the right seats on the bus filled with the right people allows the bus to go down the road. I can be on a different bus or an airplane going someplace else.

As to mistakes I made and learnings from those that can help other people - right off the bat, keeping somebody on the team that should be let go today. I'm a nice guy; I want to please everybody—my clients, my employees. I'll give everybody a second and third or fourth or fifth or sixth chance. The last thing I want to do is put somebody on the street. But there's a problem I've had for a number of years. When it was time for somebody to go, I just didn't have the big boy pants to do it. Maybe somebody's got some kind of personal issues that are somehow adversely affecting other people on the team or something, and not addressing those. Chris is a facilitator and a coach and my other business partners certainly have encouraged me and held me accountable to having conversations sooner than later. There's another thing, being accountable. A lot of us sole owners can go through life without being accountable to anybody, and to have somebody who's actually interested in seeing you do well and agreeing to be accountable to them, is a very important thing.

There is another thing I've learned in business which can be a big problem for people. I served four years on the Supreme Court Office of Attorney ethics as a senior public member. What I saw in the complaints that came to the ethics office were attorneys and licensed professionals that did not respond in a timely fashion or respond well to their clients. As I take a look at my own profession, I see surveyors and engineers who have discovered that maybe they've made a mistake, and they didn't address that right away with their clients. It could grow into something that could cost them a lot of money with lawsuits, or even lose their license or be reprimanded. I know from watching all this, in my experiences, if I actually make a mistake on some project, I get a hold of the client immediately. I say, I'm sorry, we've just discovered that we've made a mistake and I'm going to make this right. The other thing is it's so good that this mistake happened because now I realize all these other things that we can improve for you now. It's going to come out of my pocket. I'm not asking you to spend any money on any of this, and we're going to make it right. But I promise you, everything's going to be better, much better than it was before.

We just recently found a mistake on a project for a client with a brand-new piece of technology. We didn't vet out the new technology well enough. We thought we understood it. There were variables that were set into the scientific instruments that we just thought the software would hold the variables that we set, as we've been doing for 30 years with other similar instruments. Well, it didn't do it. The data went out that was wrong. That could have been problematic for the client. I got a hold of the client immediately. I told him what happened. I said, we will rectify this. And if it costs you any money at your end, I certainly will cover those costs. Furthermore, you don't have to pay my bill. Three weeks later, they paid our bill. Be as honest as you can with your employees, as honest as you can be with your clients. Don't try to snow your clients; don't try to give them a line of crap. If you can't do something, tell them you can't do something. Then you'll be able to work through something with them that they don't know how to do. Figure it out together – how to have resources be involved in and associations that are similar to your profession. For a number of years, I'd be on a weekly teleconference call with people from Anchorage to Jerusalem. You know, you think about all the people in between, the resources around the world.

I had some friends or family members or colleagues who have passed away. They may have had businesses and left their spouses and/or their businesses in kind of disarray. I wanted everybody in my company to be taken care of. I had another friend who had a heart attack; he had to shut down his business the next day. All of his employees couldn't pay the bills or put food on the table the next day. That's never going to happen here. Chris introduced me to somebody else who was involved with our Bus at the time – an attorney who was very well versed in succession planning and businesses and estates. So I have a plan in place that if I were to get run over by the Lake Land bus, it'll just be like there's a speed bump in the road; the company will continue to operate. The clients are just going to think I'm going to be away on an extended ski vacation. A sale of a business is nothing that you want to do in a month or a six-month timeframe. You really want to spend time and think about who gets affected by it financially, and how you get affected by it. What's the benefit to you, a spouse, the people that work for you, your business partners, etc? Have a succession plan in place while you're really healthy and alive. That is a really good thing. It's the time to do it.

CARYN LEE
OWNER OF NARRATIVE

I have been a small business owner for 14 years now, after a 15-year corporate management consulting career. I bought into my first company with two partners. We grew from 5 to 11 employees and added 24 global distributors. I sold my shares back to them and started Narrative in 2015. Narrative is a boutique consulting company focused on partnering with our clients to develop, hire, engage, and retain their people. We use researched-based assessments in much of our work, one of which is a proprietary personality assessment, the Narrative Big Five Assessment. I categorize my clients as "whales" (those I work with consistently over the course of a year or more), "dolphins" (those who I work for once or twice a year on a specific project, such as team building, conflict resolution, or coaching), and "minnows" (one off projects such as career coaching). At the time that I joined The Bus, I had one whale that I'd worked with for about two years. Before that whale, my business was made up mostly of dolphins. I knew I could not be successful on just dolphins and minnows. Before,

I had several dolphins, but it wasn't a sustainable business. Having a whale was great, but what if this whale just swims away? I knew that I had to engage more whales. At the same time, I didn't know exactly how I was going to market or sell to them. Now we have three whales that make up about 80% of our effort and income. And I've added people to the team to provide more services.

I engaged my new clients through referrals. All my business is referrals. With whales, if you do a good job, they're going to keep you and they're going to tell their friends and colleagues what you have done for them. I also have referral partners that get to know my work and refer me to their clients. My Bus helped in several ways:

- It forces me to look at my numbers every month.
- They continue to push me to engage whales and to keep developing business.
- They push me to realize that if I want to grow, I have to have more team members. I'm still working on that, having more people to work in the business so I can work on the business.

It's great, because I now have an administrative partner and three people who can interpret the assessment for clients and assist clients in multiple ways.

The changes I've been making involve getting more referrals, diversifying the clients so that I'm not too invested in one, looking at the numbers monthly, and then getting additional help so that I can be freed up to focus on taking care of the whales and getting more whales. That has changed my business. For example, I increased my revenue by 60% both of the last two years.

What has that done for my life? Well, my husband is talking about retiring because he thinks I'm making enough money. I'm totally fine with that. If he will take over more of the household management and family responsibilities, that works out great for me. I love what I do and am happy to spend time working. I have more stress – not financial stress, but I'm working too much right now. The goal, and what Chris is helping me with, is to keep me focused on getting more help, because with that I can grow, but also figuring out how much I want to work. Right now, I work six days a week. I go home, have dinner with the family, maybe watch my guilty pleasure, a crime drama, then I go back to work from about 10 pm to 1 am. Not every night, but most nights. Some nights, it's just until 12. Some nights, it's 1 and sometimes it's 2. Also, I work four to six hours on Sunday. I don't mind doing that, but I don't want to do it long term.

I am working on a plan to be able to get rid of the night work. First is building a sustainable team. Some of it is getting a little more organized – a little more efficient with certain things. I'm not a spring chicken. I'm almost 57. I started over at 50. I sold my shares to my previous company; I thought I was going to buy my partners out and continue to grow that 11-person company with 24 distributors. Instead, they ended up buying me out. I'm totally happy because I plan to work for at least another 10 years, but it is taxing after a while. I'd rather not work at 12 o'clock at night. The buyout situation was unexpected. It was a switch. There were a lot of bumps on that road! It was like a divorce because for 10 years we worked together almost every day. I have a 12-minute, Ted-like talk on that. I call it, "How I lost my business." It's on Youtube.

I knew I could pick up and do what I needed to do, but it was the hardest from an emotional perspective. It was not the result I wanted or intended. Now it's fine. I'm happy where I am and I'm really glad that I built Narrative. Building Narrative was a very humbling experience because I'd always been successful. I was an associate partner with a big management consulting company. Then I grew that other business. So, I thought, I'm sure I can start a new business and make it successful. But the first three years were so much harder than I ever thought they would be. I often say, I thought I was special and it wouldn't take me the three to five years that everyone told me it takes to build a business.

There were some roadblocks or obstacles in those first three years. I thought, I'll just go out and talk to my network. I have a huge network. Some of my old clients will surely come with me. One day, people took my call and the next day, they did not. It was the weirdest and most crushing aspect. My clients that I had all these relationships with – one day I was their best buddy and the next day I couldn't get them on the phone. That was another really good lesson – that you can't control everything; you can only control your actions and your words and what you do, and you can't control anybody else's actions. That was hard.

I thought - I'll go to my network, tell them I have this business and then clients will come. It didn't work that way. I didn't have a lot of trouble selling before. And I thought I liked sales. When you have a new business, you have to narrow your products and services and focus on a specific audience. I was spraying and praying, and it just takes a long time to get focused on what it is exactly that you're selling, how you sell it, how you get people to understand they need it, and how you get to the right people. I was doing a lot of networking with potential referral partners; I had to get to where I talked to the prospects, the people that were going to write me a check. You've got to find who they are and start to build a relationship. Relationships take a while to build. I thought I was special because my business was profitable in a short period of time. Turns out I'm not so special. I do think persistence was the key. I refused to give up even though my husband wanted me to go back to the corporate world so many times. I was not going back. I refused to even think about going down that road. If I did, I couldn't concentrate on the goal. I was convinced this was going to work. It just took longer than I thought it should.

Besides miscalculating the time that it would take, there were other mistakes I have made that could benefit other business owners – with the things I learned from those mistakes. One was spending too much time networking in the wrong places with people that were not going to hire me. Also, though I didn't know who my audience was, I knew who I thought they were. It took me a long time to figure out I'd have to work with so many dolphins to make a decent living. I know it sounds crazy. It sounds stupid now, but I thought I knew who my clients were. Narrative's services can be helpful to any company of any size. It doesn't matter. But you can't market it that way. You have to market it to specific types of clients. Clients want specialists.

When you start working with small to middle market companies, you realize how much they don't know. I've worked with large corporations, such as Accenture, Bank of America, and Wells Fargo. Clients need so much help with communication, employee engagement, conflict resolution; there's a great deal of opportunity. It's finding those people who are in pain and letting them know how you can help them. That's one of the hardest parts of what I do – explaining to people what I do.

I did struggle with my messaging, but I am overcoming that. The people who refer me now know. Today I talked to a new president three months into the job. She has inherited a leadership team who have been with the company for a long time. My referral partner is a good friend of the new president and recommended me. This referral partner introduced me to another client over a year ago. That client was also a new president, who had a new CFO and the rest of the leadership team had been at the company for over 20 years. My referral partner had a story to tell about my success with that leadership team. So, she told her friend, and now this prospect wants me to work with her team. Notice they are both women. My current three whales have male presidents. I'm excited to work with a female president. Just to note that there are many women in senior leadership roles at my other clients and many of my dolphins are led by women.

I am building a track record. Stories are what people need to know. Stories sell. It can become very specific. In the example above, the story is that I can help teams with new leaders. It's all about people and getting up to speed quickly with understanding who you are working with. It allows the team to become very productive very quickly. With each service, I have client success stories to tell.

The messaging is still hard. Thank goodness, now I have people referring me and I don't have to just go into a networking group and give a pitch. I've actually ditched the pitch. I just give examples of my client work.

I value Chris and the Bus. I really like having Chris as a coach because he pushes me to focus on the big picture. We get along really well; we click, and he helps push me to think about the things that I'm not addressing. A lot of times my head is in the weeds because I'm actually doing the client work. I need to work more on my business than in my business and that is why I've added people to the team. I need to think in terms of the team and Narrative, rather than me. I also love collaborating and that is where the Bus comes in. They are great people and we care about each others' success. They also point out the obvious things I may be missing.

Julbert Abraham
of AGM

I am originally from Haiti and came to the United States about 23 years ago. I've been an entrepreneur since I was 18. When I was in college, I had a small business with my friends, where we did event photography, and partnered with the local schools and universities. Through that, I learned a lot of different skill sets. After I graduated from college, I decided to exit that business and started working in corporate America. Fast forward, I got laid off and started a marketing consulting business where I used LinkedIn® to find clients for myself. Then I enrolled into an MBA program. After I graduated, I noticed there was a need for business owners to learn how to use LinkedIn®, so I started this business part time, and began slowly going full time.

I met Chris at a Chamber of Commerce event, and I had heard so much about him, this guy that's sending so many people referrals. I needed to meet this guy. He invited me to a small event where he was working with business owners, where they get a chance to share some of the challenges that they were having. At the end, he said, if you want more help, we can help and here's the investment. I just started my business; that investment was a whole lot of money to me at the time. So, I said," I'll let you know." I never got back to him. One random day I noticed that he sent me a text.

Before I got On The Bus™, I had no idea what I was doing, and I had no direction of where I was going. I knew I wanted to have a business. Even though I had a business MBA, I still didn't know what I was doing, and I had no clarity. The only thing I knew was, I wanted to do six figures because that was what everybody was striving to do. I experienced a lot of challenges. I didn't have any processes or any systems; I didn't really have team members; I didn't really have structure. Business is really about having systems and structure, but I didn't have any of that. The only thing I had was that I knew I had a potentially good product, and I knew I can sell the heck out of it. I didn't really have a structure where I can actually grow the business where I can take it to over multiple six figures and seven. I didn't have that belief and didn't have mentors that could teach me how.

After I got On The Bus™ and started to work with Chris, a lot of things changed. One, being around the right people – people who have already done what I'm looking to do. Chris did an awesome job putting me around those quality people. I am super grateful for it. Second, having an accountability team. If you said you're going to do one thing, you better come back and have it completed because that's your word. Having that team to support you is huge. Chris was great at giving ideas that you didn't think about before. He was really good at listening, and really helps you come up with ideas. By being part of the Bus, it helped me change the way I do business. It actually helped me thrive.

Now my life and my business are a blessing. One big thing, I got married. Business is thriving, growing into several multiple six figures. Some of the stuff that I used to have on my post-it note as the amount of money I wanted to make has come to reality. It helps me evaluate my company consistently. On The Bus™ gave me a lot of the foundation that I needed, at the time as an entrepreneur coming up and not knowing one thing from another – stuff that you couldn't learn in an MBA program.

As far as the successes I now have, there are more clients, we have a team – we have an international team in four different continents. We have a structure, we are meeting our goals, we've surpassed some of our goals. We've helped a lot of other businesses improve their competence.

Focusing for a moment on mistakes I made that could benefit other business owners, and what I learned from them – one mistake I made is sometimes growing too fast and without having clarity in my vision. It can be detrimental to growth. We hear you have to grow and growing has different facets. Growing a business can be in sales but growing a business can be in a team and can be a lot of different facets. One of my mistakes was I wanted to grow so fast that I had to call on too many team members at a faster pace than necessary, and that impacted the quality of the service that we were providing. Instead of helping us, it hurt us. Also, something that I've learned, you can make mistakes and if you're upside down on your finances, you can reverse it. If you need to let people go, don't wait too long. That's another mistake. I remember one time when I was in one of our Bus meetings, and I said I need to let this person go. Everybody suggested I need to do it fast. I waited a month. That lost us $20,000 to $40,000 in business by waiting. Hire slow; fire fast. It's the truth.

Don't be afraid to let people know that you need help. I think a lot of us are too proud to let people know what we're struggling with. That's something we all have to work on. You have to be willing. If you want help, you have to sometimes be transparent. One thing I love is we were able to share each other's numbers, so we knew where we were. Don't be afraid to share your challenges with people because they can help you. Your ego can kill you sometimes. You make mistakes. You have to fix them.

MARK THE VIDEO GUY

We're a video production company. I always liked photography. My dad had a dark room in our house when I was a kid, so I was always thrilled with the magic of making photos, and I always loved movies. Through college I took a couple of TV classes and then at County College, I majored in broadcasting, and I took as many TV and photo classes as I could. Then I moved on to William Paterson University with the same thought process in mind, with a film emphasis. When I was a high school kid, I was a metalhead music guy, and I didn't really care about high school. Even during the first couple years of college, school wasn't really my thing, but I knew I needed to do something. When I went to William Paterson, that's where I got serious about filmmaking. When I graduated in 1997, technology was very different back then. It's not like it is today. Everybody's got a camera on a phone now.

I graduated and the world still seemed very big to me – like, how do I know how to make a career out of this? How do I do this? I'm either going to move to LA or maybe I could try to stay in New York. I was doing so much film stuff, and I was a little burned out when I graduated, and I needed a break. But I will come back to this; this will be my career. I just don't know how yet. I was in a band; I just played music for a year or two. Then technology started to come around in 1999.

I was always self-motivated. I got a job as young as you can, bagging groceries. I always wanted to be the best. Maybe the best way is to just do this ourselves. From playing in bands, we knew a lot of bands were on MTV or VH1. These hardcore bands were able to make music videos. So, I turned to my business partner, Tom, and said, "Let's start a music video production company." And because a camera came out that was more like filmmaking, not so much video in 1999, I hit my dad up and he gave us a little bit of seed money. We went out and bought a camera and all of a sudden, we're in business with no clients and not really knowing anything about business. But we had desire. Well, we're gonna figure it out as we go. And I'm gonna give it everything I have. The first couple of years were very trying. If somebody needed to see something, I ran off a VHS copy and mailed it to them. There was no putting it online and getting an answer back in five minutes. It was like a day's process. We started the company, and we were just trying to do anything and everything. We got a couple of jobs; we took phonebook ads out and we just got a couple of clients. Then we started doing weddings and became very successful at that, although that was not what we wanted to do.

One of the first business challenges was that we were doing something, we were making some money, but it was the exact opposite of what I wanted to be doing. I had to make a decision to stop it and try to get back to doing what we started. The first couple of years were very rough without having some business knowledge; it was difficult to figure stuff out as we were going. We had some successes and a lot of peaks and valleys. Our third partner left because we were inconsistent and not making money. We hit a point where we had a couple of decent clients. Early on, we had a mentor who became one of our first clients – a financial planner. We had a little bit of a business guru guiding us along early in our career, and I've always then been open to someone who knows more than me, if they can help me out. He helped out a lot. We had to hit this challenging period. He said all businesses hit this critical period at some point. He told us to go talk to other business owners about their critical period and how they got through it. Sure enough, we did. We would take people out for lunch, and dinner, and just let them talk about how they became successful or got through critical periods of their business. That was a huge help. One person told me I should read this book called *The E-Myth®*, and that book leads up to almost where we met Chris Lipper. That book changed our lives. It's very much about working on your business, not in your business. It felt like it was written for us at that exact moment in business for a couple of years. I felt like 95% of that book was written for me. Sometimes you can take 5% out of a book, or sometimes you take 90% out of a book. That book was a game changer. That's where we first started saying we need to find an editor, so we're not working everyday editing, and we can work on the business more.

Then, all of a sudden, we met Chris, who was forming his groups at the time, and it just seemed to make sense. We're starting to hire employees. Why not talk to other business owners about what they're doing? Talk to other people and hear their successes and hear the failures they learned from and try to apply it to what we're doing. That was a saving grace talking to mentors, reading a bunch of books, including *The E-Myth®*, and then meeting Chris.

We encountered challenges – first was just how to get more clients, then we started hiring people, so now we have employees, and that begins to change the dynamic. Going on my first Bus, I liked being with people from almost the same size business as mine and dealing with some of the same challenges. How do I grow and get more clients? How do I begin to manage some of these employees? It's things you didn't even think you needed to do; you have to have this set up, or even get an employee agreement. I'm switching my mentality. I'm a creative guy. I want to be a director. That's why I started this company, but now I have to be a business owner and spend time on the other side of this. When I first started the company, I didn't know anything about business. I just knew I was passionate about making this work.

Once I started to work with the other people On The Bus™ and get their feedback, a lot changed. I had one employee who was a salesperson, and he had a lot of issues. He was a great salesperson, but I had a lot of issues with his appearance or certain other things. How do I go talk to this person? How do I get them to not do this and do that? Even on the legal side of it, such as, creating an employee handbook saying this is the way you need to dress, and to get them to sign something that acknowledges that. A lot of that started to be a big help to us, to do it the right way when it comes to legalities. Also, the Bus members help you be accountable. I like the accountability. I come in with a challenge. They say, by next session, you need to have that employee handbook written. The accountability level helped to be able to keep on track, then to grow the business. I also like to be able to give feedback in that situation, and even hear myself talk about something else as well. I realize I should be doing what I'm telling them to do! I'm giving this advice, but it's something I should be implementing in my business. It just helped us get to the next level.

Then I switched to a bigger Bus; when we were making more money, I kind of outgrew the other one. Here the businesses were making more money, had more employees, and then you started dealing with the challenges on that next level. For example, micromanaging people or being able to let go. I wish I could just do something, because nobody does it the way I want to do it, but you have to let go; you can't control everything. That was a big challenge for me. I've always had about 15 things in the fire, and I'm always trying to juggle things and why can't everybody else do this? Why can't everybody else think like me and be like me? Okay, you have to calm down. The experience also helped me to not have 15 things on the burners at a time – as well as trying to prioritize the most important things. I learned to try not to be unrealistic with things that you're trying to move forward. You can't be successful moving all 15 things forward in one month; it's just not going to work. The Bus helped me to look at things more realistically and set more realistic goals.

There were other mistakes I made along the way that you learn things from. I had a business partner and he left two years ago. Like any relationship, whether it's a marriage or whatever, you learn from each other. When you're in business for 20 years, we peaked at different levels. I always struggled with how I should deal with him. We're making the same amount of money. We're equity partners, but we're not doing the same amount of work, or we don't think the same. He was a big challenge for me because he was my best friend. Friendship and business don't mix. Business is business and friendship is friendship, but I had a hard time trying to change our relationship. It's like, are you going to do something about it or shut up about it? For three months, I'd stay quiet and then something else would happen. It was just something I always struggled with. It was difficult because I guess we grew apart and then I felt more like he knew it. He didn't want to disappoint; he worked hard. I'd approach him with issues, and I always felt like we had this parent/teenage son relationship. I'd say something, and I'd see him gloss over.

If I would do it again, how would I deal with a business partner? I was glad to have one, but I should have listened to my Bus members a little bit more. They were saying the right thing, but I had a hard time implementing it because I let the friendship just get too close. I couldn't tell him he would have to take less money because it would have probably destroyed our working relationship even. That was very difficult; that was my biggest challenge. I do a lot of one-to-ones with Chris, too. And that was very beneficial

– to have The Bus and the one-to-ones where you can dig a little deeper into something, and also be accountable. I've always enjoyed Chris Lipper and the thought process behind his approach. It was also take it or leave it. It's like reading a book; sometimes the advice would hit you 90% and sometimes you may want to get one little thing, but that one little thing could be a bit of a game changer if you go implement it. With the one-to-ones, he may say something like, "no, I don't agree with it," but it just gets the juices flowing and gets the thought process going. You may take a piece of advice and not agree with it. Then two months later, all of a sudden, it does make sense and you can go implement something.

For me, the culture was also very big at our company. We're a creative company, doing video production and trying to maintain that creative culture, but not letting it get too fun. There's also that level of culture becoming too fun, and how you're perceived by people versus what you're trying to create. Just trying to create a culture and running that by a Bus, trying to find the right balance of culture, professionalism, and fun. That was also something that we really skated a line trying to implement.

After all of that experience, working with the group and peer advisory, and Chris, now things are different. Earlier, we had to let people go when we hit another critical period, even though we were successful. That was kind of a reset. My partner and I always put everybody else first; we were last. I think you need to have that mentality as you're growing a company, as owners. But we said we have to try to grow this better; we have to be a part of the growth financially as well. We may have to not get so close and be so cool. That was a learning experience.

As we grew, again, we looked for different people. We found our boundaries of where our relationships should be with people. I also learned to deal with my partner, and I brought in a COO. I had to start listening to myself and say, "Stop expecting this partner to be something he's not." As we began to grow, it was a different kind of growth. It was better and we were at a point right before the pandemic, where we employed 16 to 17 people and our mentality was we want to dominate. If there's a video going, I want it, but with that thought process you have to keep feeding this machine and make sure you're bringing it in. Sometimes it was work that you didn't even really love to do. But we had to do it, because I have employees and I have to keep this machine going.

We were about to hire a couple of people right before the pandemic, then the pandemic hit and we had to take a time out and pull it back. We pulled it way back. Sure enough, my business partner, by July of 2020, left the business. He decided to go do his own thing. I think it was just the time that you were able to reset, retool your thought process. It was bittersweet because we had worked together for 21 years. But at the same time, it was a bit of a relief because something had to change. I hate to say this, but I'm happy the pandemic happened from the business perspective – not for people getting sick or dying – but the pandemic was actually a beautiful thing for the company because he left, and I retooled the whole business. I said, "I don't want to do it like this anymore." And the pandemic actually allowed me to have fewer people here. I don't have to get all this business for the machine. And I actually can work a little less and have a better work life balance. I'm actually making more money and I don't have to have as much stress as I had before. It was a little bit of an eye opener. There's 20 years in business and having the clients who we have helped. But I didn't have to worry if we lost a couple when the pandemic hit.

What has now changed for me is that I don't want to get back to what I had; I don't need an office; I don't need 16 to 17 people; I don't feel the need to dominate. I've been there, and it was fine, we did that. But it just changed. You find really good people, which I have, do really good work, and maybe be a little bit more selective in the work that you're doing. I'm actually a lot happier. The foundation from going through all that stuff still exists – the systems we've created and the way we got our systems in place, now supports where we're at. We have a really solid foundation of systems. We're good at what we're doing now and I'm a lot happier. Now the plan is to continue having that work life balance; to be a little more selective in our client base and do the work that we'd rather be doing.

I don't need to feed this machine as much as I did. And my business partner is not here anymore and I'm not dealing with that stress. I'm very happy the way things are right now. But with that said, I had a challenge with my former partner come up, and I called somebody from our old Bus as I maintain relationships with them. I said, "I have a challenge I need to bounce off of you..." You still have to have a support system; you still have to be able to reach out to people. Challenges still come up that you don't know how to handle. He was so open to helping me with that challenge. You don't know everything. You don't even know the best way to handle everything all the time. You need a support group.

Mike Doyle
Animator-in-Chief at Drive 80

I've been pretty much a solo person; I don't want to work for anybody except myself. When I was younger, I had my first business partnership when I was in a band. We graduated high school; we didn't want to go to college. Let's just get a van and tour. So, we did that for two and a half years. That was my first taste of a business partnership without actually knowing it. We didn't have the fundamentals at 19, such as all four of us having the same goal. It's the same as business – do we have four different opinions here? How do we organize this and go in the same direction, because we want to keep playing music? When that fell apart, it was the beginning of a lesson – now I never work with partners.

That ended and I just fought this whole thing; I want to figure something out where one day I am working for myself. That led to moving to California from New Jersey. Then I found graphic design, but I realized I had to put myself through school, so I came back and followed my gut, basically. When I'm asking for things, kind of putting it out there in the universe, it's like, I really want to do this. I don't know how to do this; I need some help. Now in life, I know how to ask for that and say okay, I really need this, and it shows up. But back then, I was kind of just winging it. So, I came back to Jersey, went to school, and paid for my own 10-month course. I started working at a job sort of freelancing and I hated it. Within that time, I started different business partnerships, and they failed. I didn't really know what business was, but I just thought, "I'm doing this and it's cool." It's going to work in my favor. People are just going to show up and buy my stuff because it's cool. That starts a whole journey.

I met Chris in 2011. At that point, I'd been freelancing for about five or six years for myself. It was just, I'll put cool stuff out there. People will find me and then I'll be successful. I'll make money. Fast forward, I started an LLC, Drive 80 Studios, which has now been around for 11 years. I built it based on, well, all these things I do. I didn't want to give it a real name, like I didn't want it to be video production in New Jersey dot com or something. I wanted to be very broad because I was going to change my mind. I left the freelancing job, which I had for four years making a ton of money, because they just cut freelance. So I was on my own. I was doing a lot of different things, so my week would be creating a banner ad, making a print ad, making a website, doing video production, and doing photography. I was using all of the skills that I had and thinking this will all make sense.

Chris suggested that I read a book called *Built to Sell*®. After the partnership ended, I decided to sell everything and travel. I took books, signed them, and gave them to friends – telling them hopefully this helps you on your journey. That book said to do one thing really well as it makes your life a lot easier. Then I'm saying to the universe, I need ideas and help again. This might sound super woo-woo, but it's weird. When you really do that, and you're asking for it and you keep your eyes open, it shows up. I asked this a lot. I really need help. At the time, I was married, and the person I was married to was starting in CrossFit®. This other guy who was starting in CrossFit® had this friend named Chris Lipper. Chris Lipper shows up to an event; he's all tied dyed out and has this Grateful Dead® look, and I walk up to him. He's super nice; just a super chill guy and laid back. I'm confused. Who's this hippie who's going to give you business advice? I was like, "Hey, man, I hear you do these mastermind groups." I found out that's what Rockefeller and Carnegie used to do. I want to be that rich, so how do I do this? He's like, "Okay, well, I'm gonna just come down and we'll talk." Then I roll in, and we sit in his room, and he just gives me the sales thing. I walk in and he was structured. Okay, this guy's for real. He tells me about this group he has where he's bringing businesses together. You go for four hours once a month and sit in this room. It is structured. Someone mediates the discussion, and each person gets 10 minutes to talk. Then they get two minutes of feedback from every single person. I immediately fell in love with it because it was so green. I had no idea what to do and I was literally the youngest person in the group. I sat in this group, and it answered the questions that I had. It was just great being facilitated with people who gave me really good advice. I loved Chris during this whole thing. I would show up at his office, just to talk about life, and looking back, I think I was definitely just burning time. But he was always open to listen to me. He really guided me. He saw what I was doing, and he would give me advice. He'd say, "you have to start networking. We're going to get you in the chamber." Any time I was stuck, I would go talk to him. And it was so helpful. I think he knew that if he put me in a setting, I would just do my thing.

Chris said, "Go to this networking thing." My response was, "What's the Chamber of Commerce?" I showed up in this room, and I'm this young dude who's not wearing a suit and everyone's wearing a suit. And he met me there and he says, "Ok, this is what you're going to do." I looked at the room and it became a challenge. I'm going to have everyone in here know my name. That's my goal. Two months later people started thanking Mike Doyle because Chris also taught me how to get referrals and how to structure a sales meeting. I can't give him all the credit, but he was literally the star – teaching me what business was, and he just pointed me in that direction. As in any mentorship, like in life, you start in one place, and then you outgrow it, but you get as much as you need and then you go to the next thing. And the next thing. Since Chris, I've had many, many, many coaches, because I saw how necessary it was in the very beginning. Any time that I feel like I'm stuck, I'm going to hire somebody who's going to help me with this one thing.

The group experience, working with the peer advisory group was like a therapy session, because working for yourself is very lonely. The growth of your company just becomes your own mind saying how far do you want to take this? I have more of a life coach now because the business is doing well. I haven't had a business coach in a long time, just because I got a little burned out with the hustle. With the group, I loved it because I would go there for a therapy session and I would just blurt out, here's why I'm stressed out; here's where I'm stuck. I remember David Derr gave me some advice. To this day, I still love it. I asked how do I take an animation and make it physical as a gift to somebody new? He said, "Why don't you just make prints of the screen capture and then send them to him in a frame, because then it's sitting on their desk. They're going to love it because it's a physical thing." No one does that nowadays. I should really get back into this because I did it for a while. They would leave it on their desk. When people come in the room, they'd be like, "Oh, what's that?" It was something I never would have thought of. You get to pick people's brains around you. I also got bookkeeping advice from people. If I needed to meet someone, someone in the group happened to actually know someone. I needed an animator at the time to take on projects. I said that out loud and this woman said, "Oh, my son's looking. He just graduated" To this day, I hire him for freelance jobs. I never would have known how to structure a team like that. Going through the meetings, they told me how I can freelance with somebody where you don't have a salary. I didn't even know this existed, even though I was doing it myself. I can hire other people, too. I just learned the minute structures of business. So many people out there give you this broad sales pitch. They make it look sexy. The story is sexy, but the day you're doing it, there's nothing sexy about it, because you're wondering what do I do today to grow this business? How do we get new clients? How do I sell? How do I manage my team? How do I project manage? You don't know what to do, so having people around you that had that experience can share it. It just opens your eyes. Because you have done it, you had the experience and I'm going to take from it whatever is going to matter to me.

I was so unstructured and now look where it took me. I've had the company for 11 years. I started off scrambled, narrowed it down to video, then narrowed it down to animation. I brought it to the group, and I said, "I had an aha moment, I'm going to just do explainer videos." It was funny, because in the group of eight, they all said, "We have no idea what this is." I said, "Trust me, this is going to work because it's one product, based on *Built to Sell*®." It said do something very simple. Because, if you could say NO way more than yes to projects, then that's just going to make your life a lot easier. So, I just made a product that is airtight.

My first explainer video was with Chris; he explained what his group was, and I just recorded him. Then I designed and animated the video. He used it for years. Then he used it in his sales pitches to get people to come into his groups, and he would lead with it. I knew I was definitely on to something. Sometimes I think I should get back into a group like that, because it is very helpful. I put too much pressure on myself for a really long time about making my company have a purpose. Once I let go of that, I was like, I don't need to be this million-dollar machine to go and drop food off at a local food bank. Why don't I do the smallest thing possible to get that aspect and help my community? I really let go of that and said, I just want this company to make a ton of money. And that's going to allow me to help my community. I think I like having the business just be a business. I've been working by myself now for 17 years. Today, I had this meeting and I have another project that will take an hour and then after that I'm just gonna do whatever the hell I want. I built this life based on, "I'm not going to kill myself over money." I have projects where they're now in the background working and a freelancer just emailed me this morning with our latest storyboards. I'm going to send it to a client and I'm good until Monday.

If I look back at what mistakes I made that I learned from and other people could also learn from, first it was bookkeeping and taxes. I thought I'd just do it differently than anyone else. But no, you have to follow the rules. Taxes and bookkeeping were a big thing with me, how to keep that organized. What else? Trying too hard to attach a purpose to my business was a big mistake that put stress on me. I moved down to North Carolina six years ago and I went through a lot of life stuff. When you're on your own, you're trying to balance life and business and you can't turn either of them off. They bleed into each other. You just make as much money as you can, because that really alleviates stress and then you have free time to do good things.

Now I can separate life and business, but it took me a very long time. How did I do it? I just stopped caring so much. I stopped believing all the crap that's been fed to me. All these books and podcasts and these idiots who are in their 20s telling you they're making millions and hundreds of millions. Is this like a fantasy they're living in? You put stress on yourself. I just started asking myself, what do I want? I don't need to prove anything to anybody else. I think in the beginning, I tried to play the game, and tried to make it for everyone else. When you're working for yourself, the number one rule is you're not doing this for anybody else, but yourself. When you lose that, you lose your own voice. I show up super laid back and kind of aggressive at times, but also tongue in cheek. But then when I get down to a project, I show up, I make deadlines – and I stress about it. That's the only stress that I allow myself. When I'm on a deadline, I'm head down, plugged in, doing my thing. I go on LinkedIn® and think it's the greatest social network ever. Everyone's so afraid to say anything. Say your opinions. If I'm paying a business coach, I'm going to listen, and I'm going to be very teachable. But if someone's giving me unsolicited advice, get out of my way.

I'm a very open book, so I don't care about sharing my personal life. I was married and I was helping her start the CrossFit® business. The person I was with ended up leaving for her business partner. I'm working for myself; I'm basically the only support that this little family had. So, there's the pressure of getting jobs because I am the sole earner and she's starting a business that I helped fund. What you don't realize in business is that life is still going to happen, and it can completely derail you. My dad suddenly passed away, and then three months later, my wife, at the time, left me. That was the biggest one two punch that can literally just destroy you and you still have to run a business. You're in the weirdest headspace. I'm two or three years into starting this LLC and I'm trying to sell. I'm trying to market; I'm losing my shit as much as possible. I ended up selling everything. I have a laptop. I work for myself. I can do this from anywhere, so I sold everything and started traveling. I stumbled upon Raleigh, North Carolina, in my travels, kept traveling, got back to New Jersey and realized

I was just over New Jersey, living there for 35 years. I'm sick of the snow. I'm sick of New Jersey. Nothing but love for Jersey, but it wasn't for me anymore. Then I came back to Raleigh. It was cool because it was a fresh start. I've been here for six years; it's very tech oriented, with a huge startup scene, and it's just exploding now with real estate, which is crazy. That's what got me here.

David Quick
Total Cover IT

I've worked in IT for about 25 years now. Before that, I was in accounting. My last full-time role was IT Director for a midsize accounting firm. I started there in 2000 and was there until the very start of 2018. While I enjoyed working at the firm, working at the same place for my entire career is not what I planned. I wanted more growth, which I wasn't finding there. Around 2004-2005, I established an arrangement with the partners where I could get my own IT consulting clients and just do that on the side. In 2008, I decided that I wanted to formalize this into an ongoing company, which later that year resulted in the creation of Total Cover IT.

Around the time when I was thinking about doing this, I started with a business coach. I went on to work with him for about eight years. While I appreciated that relationship and it gave me value, he was getting out of business toward the end of our time together. He was tapering off and had secured a full-time job. By 2016, I was actively looking for somebody else and he encouraged it. I originally met Chris when I joined the Chamber of Commerce in 2014. He was an ambassador, so it was his job to call on the members and then introduce us to the chamber, be a resource and such. In late 2016, Chris sat next to me at a monthly Business Connections event, and we reconnected. It was the right person at the right time. We talked; we had a one-to-one and I signed on with his group, called On The Bus™.

By 2017, my flexible arrangement with the firm was growing harder and harder to maintain due to the demands of the job, so it was apparent that I was coming to a decision-point about staying with my job or going into the business full-time or finding another job. I ultimately decided to go into the business full time. There were a couple of reasons. One, toward the end of my employment, although it was a nice place to work, I didn't feel there was growth there and my flexible arrangement was diminishing to the point where it felt like a "normal" job. I'm sure if I got another IT job somewhere else, it would probably feel like a "job" as well. I would do the work. And there's no variety. I'll be sitting in a room, just doing my work all day, and I'll go home at the end of the day. It would be more of the same that would just be more drudgery. I didn't see myself just working at an office or working on servers for the next 20 years, just for one company. What interested me in having a business was that it provided stimulation. It wasn't just working for one company; I was doing work for a variety of different companies. It's always interesting seeing different types of businesses, learning about the businesses, trying to solve their IT problems, and trying to help them to get more out of their IT to help their business. I felt I was making more of an impact than I could have made working for a company. There's that aspect and also the potential growth opportunity for me both professionally as well as financially. If you're the owner of a business, you can take it as far as you want, so there's no limit. You can build this to a few million dollars if you want to, versus IT in a regular job, you're probably not going to do that.

In the beginning, the challenge was figuring out how to get started and figure out what kind of business, because it wasn't necessarily a foregone conclusion that I was going to do IT work. It just was the first thing out of my head. My business coach at the time and I felt I'd like to do managed services. The thought was, how do we do that? How do we get started and how do I get the resources I need to deliver on the services I provide? I originally went the franchise route. I thought that was like a good business in a box, so to speak. Being process oriented, that seemed like a good option. I don't know if I would say that was one of my biggest mistakes, but it was a lot of money out the door and it had its own challenges. The expectation was they're going to deliver on the back end. The problem was they did not to the degree that was satisfactory. It presented a lot of challenges and it didn't seem like they were very organized. In their marketing, they first said to go after very large companies that have 50 or more employees and then they said go after small companies. I was constrained by their model, what we can charge, and how to present proposals. Long story short, we moved away from that; I only had a five-year agreement, so we phased that out. It was funny because when I first organized my business structure in 2008, we decided the name for the business and kicked a few things around. We were going to be operating under the franchise, so it really didn't matter. I don't know how I came up with Total Cover IT; it seemed like a weird little name – it just seemed odd at the time. I came up with a couple others, one or two of which I actually liked better but they were not quite as unique. Ironically, it was my business coach who talked me into using Total Cover IT. It was perhaps very fortunate that I selected Total Cover IT when I decided not to operate under the franchise anymore.

In restarting, getting away from the franchise, I had to do all the things that the franchise was at least trying to do. For me on my own, like a back end, there are certain tools that you need to deliver on that service. I had to be able to find those on my own and evaluate them and choose which ones are the right ones. These are all things that are free that an IT franchise does for you. That also meant a marketing program. Typically, they'll train you on the whole model from soup to nuts. They have the tech side support as well as the marketing side. You're going to have more structure as to exactly what you need to do from start to finish. And I didn't have any of that, so I had to figure out all that stuff on my own.

It was apparent that I needed to make a change when my other business coach transitioned out of his business. The relationship tapered off over time.

I had some trepidation. I often wondered, because I was so dependent upon that one-to-one relationship with him, what would happen if I didn't have him anymore? How would I run my business? That literally kept me awake at night. I didn't know what I would do if I didn't have him.

When I joined Chris' program, On The Bus™, what appealed to me about the peer group model was that I didn't just have Chris. I had a group of other business owners that I can share my challenges with. Chris has a whole community around him, not just the accountability group, which was the core, but also Chris has a whole ecosystem around him of events like a trade show and sales training. You get to interact with other people. The changes I experienced when I joined were not as much from a monetary standpoint, but from my personal growth. I developed more confidence through interactions, not only with Chris, but with my fellow business owners and other people On The Bus™. I got more confidence in being able to make decisions. I had the realization I'm not the only one with these challenges and I'm able to share with my On The Bus™ group. Likewise, I was able to share my experience with them for their challenges.

It made me more energized, to think more about being a business owner. As a result of that, I gained more confidence in making my own decisions for my business. All of that trepidation went away. I feel confident that I can carry on the business, regardless of circumstances, because of that – not that I would want to stop working with Chris or the group. But I've grown to a point where I feel that I have more control.

Acquiring customers is one of the main challenges that any business has. That was my challenge throughout. Particularly, it was in the early days when I was still working full time, so that made it very challenging. It's been a long process; I'm starting to see the fruits of that growth. The growth seems to be leading to more confidence and it seems to be resulting in me being able to interact with prospects and I am more confident with them. Even though I had an accounting background and had experience, I still felt like I didn't know as much as I needed to know about running a business when I got On The Bus™. I felt I needed something, and I didn't feel like I could operate without somebody there for me. At the time, I was thinking in terms of a business coach.

Considering mistakes, to some extent, the franchise may have been a mistake, even though there was some value in it. If I had had my board, or Bus, as we call it, at the time, and I presented that idea to them, they may have all pushed me away from it right from the get-go. Why should I be investing upwards of $10,000? I also, more recently, invested in a marketing program and my group had some resistance to that idea. I didn't really follow them. I just went with it anyway. Maybe it was okay for the short term, but maybe I think I stayed there too long, and I spent a lot of money that could have been better served towards other things. Maybe if I had not stayed in and followed their advice, or at least, restricted the duration of that, I may have been in a better place financially. Now, when I'm contemplating a major expense, $10,000 or more, or even $5,000 or $6,000, I've got to tell the other party that I have to run this by my board before I can make any decisions on their proposal. That's now my automatic answer to any vendor, for any kind of a large expenditure.

Other things that I've learned along the way… Generally, you need to be resilient if you're going to get started in business. It's not a bed of roses.

If it were, everybody would be doing it. If you want stability, go get a job working for somebody else. In business, you're going to have a lot of challenges. There's a lot of risk, but risk can be managed. There's much greater reward than working in a job. You're going to get frustrated. On some days, you wonder why you got into the business, you get hit with some major challenge, and you don't know what to do. You may just give up. Or you may just not want to do what you're committed to doing. That's what the Bus does for me because I hit these walls, not doing the things I should be doing. I have some accountability to that Bus. If I get hit with something that's very challenging, I'm not on my own. If you're standing on your own, you may waiver and give up or scale back and not pursue it anymore. The Bus allows me to stand tall against all this adversity that's out there, so I know that I'm not on my own. You have to be resilient and stand strong and be persistent In business.

Jeannie Assante
Serial Entrepreneur

I got started in business because my husband died so many years ago when my children were very young. I found that working for somebody else was not conducive to being a single mom, so I started searching. I didn't mind working if I was sick, I didn't mind going in if I was having a challenging day, but when something was going on with one of my kids, I wanted to be off, and I didn't want to hear that I couldn't take off. There were a lot of challenges with that. In many arenas, a guy who runs a business just wants his work done, and he doesn't really care what's going on in your personal life. A lot of times when I went for a job, I found that being a woman, especially as a single parent – they really shied away from hiring me, even though I had proven my record to get my work done. Maybe not as conventionally as they wanted it done, but I got it done. Maybe I wasn't in the office, five days a week, 12 hours a day; maybe I didn't give up holidays and weekends; maybe my son's birthday was more important than getting whatever you want me to get out that morning. But

I got it out that morning. I just did it overnight. But it just wasn't what they wanted. It didn't matter if it was a man or a woman. Women were even harder than the men to work for because they felt they had something to prove being a boss.

So, I realized really quickly that working for somebody else wasn't – never mind making me happy. Happy was never in the equation, because we weren't taught that we had to be happy when we work. We just had to make money. But I realized really quickly that my kids were going to miss out on a lot and I was going to miss out on a lot. So how do we go forward with this? Getting married was one of the choices. Find a nice guy who's willing to take on your kids and you work part time to take care of whatever incidentals because that's what they did back in the day. But then you were miserable, and your kids were miserable. At the same time, that made a big difference at work because I seemed "single," because I didn't bring anyone around, and the wives were very upset because there was a single woman among the mix. So that made it even harder for me to work. I said, "I'm not doing this," so I opened up a daycare. I started taking care of other people's children. Because it was something I could do without training; I was already trained for it. I had a daycare for a very, very long time. The challenge with that was that I was working somebody else's schedule. If they couldn't take off work, I couldn't take off work. I had licensing, insurance – all kinds of crazy things. I was only allowed a certain number of kids. I was limited with my income, unless I opened up a major daycare, and now you're talking more money.

In the turmoil of all that happening, and the craziness of all that happening, I tried different businesses as well. I had a trucking company and one time I ran actually 20 some trucks. I had a man in the front of that business because I wasn't allowed in the door. Something went wrong. A guy stole one of my trucks. Now we had to go looking for the truck with the product in it. Well, guess who had to show up? Because I was the owner of the trucks. When they found out there was a woman, that was a problem. I was actually told when I walked into the office, that I'm a woman and I need to be barefoot and pregnant and chained to a stove, not in this business. That only made me want to do business more because I'm that kind of person that says, "if you're not going to let me do this, now I have to do it." Not only did I have to do it, but I had to succeed at it. So, I did it for a very long time. But it took a lot of my time, 12 to 14 hours a day, seven days a week, and my goal was just to spend more time with my kids, not less. I ended up selling that business, which was great. I made some nice capital; I was able to sustain myself for a little bit. I went back to waitressing because that's what I did for a really long time. It was easy money for me; I knew how to do it. I worked overnight; I was home during the day with my kids. Again, I was working for somebody else. In the restaurant business, back in the day as a waitress, especially if you're single, you will kind of pray to the owner. They always had a cot downstairs. If you didn't want to visit, you probably didn't have a job for much longer if you said no. I can't tell you how many times I said no and how many times I was fired.

This was not the life I wanted to lead anymore, so I started different businesses. Mary Kay was one of them. I became very, very successful, made a lot of money and I was able to work my own hours, which was fantastic. I got a free car every two years. I'd get a new car and didn't have to pay insurance. I ended up buying a house in the midst of it, which was really great. I couldn't do that before because I was too busy working. Then I realized that if a good portion of the world went broke, and they couldn't pay for makeup, that would be a problem for me. So, I said I need to find something else to do. I found many other things to do, kind of off the cuff, and they worked for a little while. Then of course they don't work after a while, and I ran by the seat of my pants. That's when I became like a bull in the China cabinet. What can I do to make money? I've got to feed my kids and keep going. I did mortgages for a while; they had their big boom, before they had the crash. I still have my Mary Kay today. I'm so happy because I built a strong customer base, which is one of my good points. Then somebody said to me that I can sell solar, and I was like, I don't know anything about solar. I don't want to sell solar; I don't want to go to school to learn about this stuff. I really didn't have to; I learned on the job, which was great, and I became extremely successful. I was one of the top people selling in the company of SunPower, which is huge, one of the top 5%. It's a worldwide company. They kept trying to get me to work for corporate and I kept saying, "Listen, you don't want me to work for a corporate man, you're going to lose a good person, because it's not my thing." I stayed in my own little world and ultimately ended up with my own company, which I still have today. I've been doing that for over 12 years.

I started doing something else in between, because I found that having multiple streams of income was a smart way to go as a single person. What if something happened to me – I fell or hurt myself or an accident? I'd be in really big trouble if I don't have some sort of residual income coming in. Everything was by sales – if I didn't sell, I didn't make money. I decided to join this company called American Communication Network, ACN. The company that they told me that I could get residual income. Now the reason that I really got excited about it was because it reminded me of Mary Kay, but with that product, there was no product to sell – there was no wishing that somebody needed lipstick. There was no wishing that somebody still needed skincare, but everybody still needs their essential services. There's no question that people are going to use gas and electricity for the rest of their lives. There's no question that people are going to use the TV and internet for the rest of their lives and their cell phones. I said, if I can make money on these products, and even just tap a small market of the people that I know, because I have a big referral source, then I would do okay and I am doing okay, which is really amazing. This money comes in no matter what happens every single month, thank God. When COVID hit, everything I had shut down, except for that. That actually raised and started making more money. It didn't cover all my bills, but it did cover a good portion. I didn't have to dip into my savings account as much as I thought.

I opened up Airbnb. Now that was quite by accident. All my children moved out. Like I said, a lot of my things are by accident; they just happened to come into my direction and I just kind of run with it. My house is always empty. I feel like it's just a waste of space, but I don't want to downsize. I like to have space. I said I'm going to get myself a roommate, but my friend just had the roommate of nightmares. She said I just started doing Airbnb, when you rent your apartment or your house or a room in your house, like you would if it was a hotel. I thought about it for a very short period of time. I ran it by my kids, just because I run everything by them, the way they run everything by me. They said to me, "You're crazy. You're going to have strangers come into your house." I ended up doing it. I loved it. I met people from all over the world and I keep in touch with a lot of them. A lot of them return when they come back. Every year. I have a lot of nurses and doctors – traveling nurses and traveling doctors. I realized really quickly that I live right by the hospital, and it was a perfect scenario. It's really big influx of referrals and returnees which is really great for me. I've got a nice little business. During COVID, the nurses and the doctors became so important. The traveling started picking back up again after that, thank goodness, because it saved me. I just got into the crypto world and I'm trying to figure that out.

I got on board with Chris and the Bus a couple of years ago. I had a coach prior to that, and it did nothing for me. I'm not sure if it was my fault, because I didn't really believe in it. That's like going to a psychiatrist and just sitting there looking at him. If you're not going to do what they tell you to do, it's not going to work. But I had a sour taste in my mouth from coaches. I said, no, this is not going to work, but Chris is very good at keeping in touch with you, and not being threatening. He's not a pusher. He's not getting in your face. Little by little, he won me over. I realized that I needed him a lot more than I thought I needed him. And now it's more like a partnership, which is really great. It's a partnership that I feel brings value.

The whole On the Bus™ peer counseling thing worked for me. One of the major things that the Bus helped me work through was how to work with people without trying to bulldoze them into a sale. That works for a lot of people, but the referrals are few and far between, even though I've gotten lucky. Because I do good work. I've had people refer people to me, but my referrals grew because I became a person that they wanted to know, instead of a person that the only time they called me is when they needed a sale. Also, the value for me from the group was that I could be myself. I didn't have to put a front up of who I was or what I was or what kind of business I was doing. If I was having a problem, I could put it out and there was no judgment, which is great. I love the idea that I wasn't judged no matter what, which is awesome. That's big, because as an entrepreneur, a solopreneur, you're always thinking somebody is judging you on what you're doing. It just made it more comfortable for me to be in my own skin, knowing that other people understand my problem. And I had the same problem, and I found a solution that I didn't think of.

I think the biggest mistake that I made was not doing a little research before I jumped into things. I've opened a lot of businesses and closed a lot of businesses before because of that. I've been successful a lot because of that too. Sometimes, when you're running fast, you're excited, but then you find out it isn't what you thought. Case in point, I realized as I was doing the cosmetic work, which I love, and I was running a huge team, that I was becoming dependent on that team selling. It became me needing them to order versus me helping them with their order. I felt very uncomfortable doing that and I realized that I really needed to get out of that market really quickly. I learned not to be such a bull in the China cabinet – not to be so forceful and not to be so needy on the sale. It'll come and have faith in the fact that it's going to come; if you just put the work in, it's going to happen.

One of the biggest mistakes I think I ever made in my entire life of working on my own is bringing on a partner, thinking that it was going to be easier to have someone working by my side. The reason that I found that to be a challenge is because I found that my work ethic and somebody else's work ethic are never going to match so I was never going to be happy. Either you have to learn to compromise, which a lot of solopreneurs cannot do, or you have to just work by yourself, which is what I love to do.

STEVE GUBERMAN
AD MAN TURNED CONSULTANT
TO THE AD FOLKS

Before I went into business for myself, I worked in-house at Panasonic for a number of years. Then I worked for a couple of small branding and design agencies. I was freelancing nights and weekends, doing the moonlighting thing. I kind of had a vision of owning my own agency one day, inspired by the agency I did internships for – the way that he ran his agency and the culture he had built. My wife and I had adopted our son, and then she got pregnant with our second child. We were living down the shore and family wouldn't come visit us for like 10 months out of the year because of the traffic. So, we decided to move to North Jersey. I said if we're going to move to North Jersey, I'm going to open my agency, because the hourly rate up here was double what it was down in Ocean County, and we were in the New York metro area. It just made perfect sense. She was able to get a job transfer, we sold our home, and had a nice nest egg to fall back on and all things just kind of aligned. Without making that decision out loud to the world we made it as a family.

One of my clients called me and said, "Hey, we want to put you on retainer." That retainer, I remember, maybe it was like 3,000 bucks a month or something like that. But at the time, that was great. It's all the money in the world for somebody just opening their doors. It was a dream that I had, but I wasn't sure how to make it happen until it finally happened. Then it was the only thing I wanted to do.

Before I got involved with Chris or On The Bus™, I had challenges and obstacles. Before I encountered him, the agency was probably two or three years old. I had a couple of employees. I know the biggest challenge that I had definitely was pipeline. Definitely cash flow. I wasn't paying myself regularly, if at all. I was not prioritizing working on the business and didn't know how to delegate and let things go – you know, to trust my team. I also had a challenging employee who I remember plaguing a lot of meetings that I had with Chris for probably the better part of a year. So, figuring out what to do and how to handle this employee was a long-term challenge of mine as well.

Once I got involved, I had to make changes. First, I was able to carve out time to work on the business. Just alone, going to the Bus meetings trained me to get out of the way and work on the business and make that a priority. I was able to learn about Disc analysis and was able to employ that on my team to find out what their strengths and weaknesses really were, how to put them in the right roles, how to communicate with them the best and how to inspire each of them. That ended up solving my employee problem, because we had her in the wrong position the whole time and that's why we kept bumping heads. Finding out what strengths and weaknesses she really had allowed me to put her into a different role that neither of us had thought of previously. It was not on anybody's radar that she should be a project manager instead of a graphic designer. Once we did that, that pretty much solved it. It helped me to charge the right amount, helped me to see the real value in what we were doing, and how to charge for it. That helped alleviate some of the cash flow challenges that I had.

People On The Bus™ would remind me, you know, to pay myself first. I think it was around that time I started working with an accounting firm instead of trying to figure it out on my own, and they helped me understand how to read a P&L, how to read a balance sheet, do proper planning and projections for taxes so that it wasn't always a scramble. It was maybe a year or two, maybe three max, that the agency really matured the most, in all those areas.

I have since sold that business. Now I am running a totally different kind of business, where I am a business coach for agency owners. Similar to Chris, I do run some mastermind groups of agency owners, and I do a lot of one-on-one coaching. But a lot of the way that I coach is based on things that I've picked up along the way through working with Chris, through books I've read, through trainings I've taken, and other coaches who I've worked with. I think it's kind of come full circle, where the experience that I had of running an agency, having the challenges of running the agency, learning the right solutions, putting those in place, and then growing the agency to a really healthy stature – that it was something that could be acquired new, it's all experience that I've been able to use with my clients now.

The experience I had with Chris and the Bus got me on the path to make the agency saleable. It certainly wasn't even close to being on my radar. I worked with

Chris in my second, third, fourth, maybe my fifth year, I think it was in the first half of my 10 years of owning the agency. Up until nine months before I sold it, I had no interest in ever selling it. My now ex-wife and I went through mediation, and I sat in that mediation and swore you were going to bury me in that agency, that I was never going to sell it and I fully believed it. It wasn't until a year later that I started to sell it. This is something I instill in my current clients. Whether you want to sell an agency or not, the stature of that agency is the same and it's just a healthy way to run a business. If you have recurring revenue, a solid team, you're not mired down in the day to day, it's profitable, the numbers are good, then it's a good healthy business. Even if you don't want to sell it, it's in the right place.

As far as some of the successes I had in the agency business, certainly, building up a really reliable, trustworthy and talented team, I think was probably one of my primary successes. I loved being able to give people jobs and help them grow in their careers. And I don't know where I picked it up, but somebody instilled in me that you want to help people mature and grow in their career to a point that they can leave, but don't want to leave. I feel like I had that with a handful of employees over the years. I had one employee who was with me, literally from in my basement. He started as an intern and employee number one and was one of the last people to leave the agency before I sold it. Ultimately, selling was a success story. Some of the clients we landed starting out, some of the first projects I did, were either a couple hundred dollars or just to get clients – and we were winning six figure contracts by the end. That just blew my mind, some of the brands that we were able to work with.

Focusing on what mistakes I might have made that can benefit other business owners, like I said, In the beginning, not paying myself, prioritizing everybody else over myself, and there's different schools of thoughts there, I firmly believe that owners don't prioritize themselves in a number of ways. I think it was a big mistake because that caused a lot of issues for me, like my personal self-worth, but also at home with my wife and my family. I think that is an important lesson that I learned that I'm glad I changed as early on as I did. That was definitely something I remember Chris helping me with –

finding the balance to work on the business versus in the business. I opened the agency because I wanted to do graphic design work, and I didn't want to work on team development or business development, or look at my numbers, I just wanted to do graphic design, I don't think that is a necessarily achievable goal, I think there needs to be a balance, so working on and working in the business. Learning to do that and figuring out the balance was important. Understanding my numbers, again, I didn't go into it thinking I needed to know how to read a P&L or balance sheet or projections or set goals or anything like that. Those were certainly big challenges. Not having everything in my brain and trusting my team to do what they're intended to do and building systems around efficiencies, as opposed to around people was a huge lesson to learn. Learning to build the system so that the people are interchangeable if they need to, certainly was a big deal. Understanding what culture is and how to build it and how intentional it needs to be. I don't think I learned that until probably year six or seven, where culture wasn't just going out for lunch, but it was really helping people grow in their career, helping them contribute to the growth of

221

the agency, giving them the autonomy to define what that meant to them and bringing that into the team.

With my new business, mistakes I have made that I learned from, and others could learn from include hesitating. I sit on ideas for way too long. When I finally launched it's like, man, I should have kicked this off a year ago. When I had the first idea, a lot of that is impostor syndrome, a lot of that is just self- doubt. But fail fast. Just try something; if it works, great. If it doesn't, who cares? Switch gears, do it again. Try things, fail fast and don't wait so long.

I read the book *Built to Sell*® by John Warrillow. It's a great book. I facilitated a group and that was one of the books that was brought up as a great topic. We were digging into it so I read *Built to Sell*® in a weekend and I'm not a big reader. In year six or so of having my agency, it helped me really rethink the way that I positioned my services and the niche that we were not in that we could have been in, as well as just change the mindset on how to pitch the services that we provided.

Although I said I wasn't really a reader, once I became one it helped to change my business. There were certainly books I've read like *Think and Grow Rich*® and *The E-Myth*® which were pivotal in my career that I would sink my teeth into. That bookshelf behind me is full of business, spiritual books for growth. A book like *Built to Sell*® pulled me in so hardcore – the fact that I got it done in a weekend when I went camping by myself and read the whole book that otherwise would have taken me a year to get through. Now we have the gift of audiobooks. I don't have to sit with a book; I can listen while I'm biking or kayaking or doing something else.

THE PICKS & SHOVELS OF INVENTING

Introduction

*"Logic will take you from A to B.
Imagination will take you everywhere." ~
Albert Einstein*

Being an inventor and having a mind that just works a little differently than most, I felt it important to recognize a different type of entrepreneur: inventors. I originally wanted to make this a third book and a stand-alone book titled *The S.O.P. for Inventing and Entrepreneurship*, but instead we will include it here in its own chapter: The Picks & Shovels of Inventing. The title comes from the gold rush, when people made their money by selling the tools versus chasing the dream. My inventing days are done – well, at least paused, as I got stung swinging for the fences. That doesn't mean that I didn't learn a ton and have some worthwhile information to share. Here we go.

I don't believe you will become an overnight success from inventing. I heard someone say once that they were an overnight success – it just took 20 years to get there. I think that inventing is very much the same and can be so fulfilling. Inventing scratches that creative itch many of us have, but can also be frustrating and heart breaking.

Here is an example of what I mean. I wanted to come up with an app you could use to play the lottery, so that instead of having to go stand in line, when there's a big amount to win, you would have a subscription. It would tell you if you won or not, and you would play whatever lotteries you want and collect your winnings.

I hired this guy, Tim, who it turns out was sued by multiple members of mine for just doing a horrible job. He said it can't be done; the government won't allow you to do it. Now, I didn't hire him for an opinion. I hired him to create the app. So first of all, he went out of bounds by giving his opinion; I didn't care about his opinion, and I shouldn't have listened to him. Years later, I was in New Jersey with no electricity due to a storm and I learned that somebody came out with something called JackPocket®. That was my idea – that happens all the time when you invent. They have a great name and it's a great product that I use for the big ones.

I had an idea for my very first invention in life when I was in kindergarten. Somebody asked if I wanted to go camping on the weekend. I was only allowed to watch TV on the weekend. I'm thinking, why would I want to go camping when I can stay home and watch TV? Then it occurred to me, I could bring a TV, but I'd have to power it. So, I came up with the idea of a portable generator. I drew a picture of a box that looked like a big car battery with six plugs on the top. Keep in mind, I'm five, right? This is kindergarten. I went to my dad and said I had this idea, what do I do? He says, "Well, you've got to bring it to somebody who can create it, who can build it." We had a friend who was an engineer type of guy. I brought him my sketch and before I knew it Honda personal generators were out in the marketplace.

I'm not taking credit for any idea, but it happens to inventors all the time. We come up with ideas thinking they are brilliant and someone is way ahead of us. Doesn't mean we should stop as we do get some gems once in a while. Invention for me, at least comes from necessity, or a whim. But that was a frustrating day when I found JackPocket® was out because I was years ahead of them. I had hired the expert to do it. I had laid it out. I listened to someone – and normally it's a motivator for inventors, when somebody says it can't be done. That's generally what motivates us – that it *can't* be done. What was his expertise? Supposedly making apps. But he didn't stay in his lane and he gave his opinion. He became a coach. This app guy gave advice he shouldn't have given. And I shouldn't have listened.

So, I sit by my fireplace thinking what if? What if I had done what I've always done and thrived off of the people around me saying no it can't be done and proving them wrong? That hasn't worked in the past as generally the first people with the idea lose money and it's the second and third who make the money on ideas. This might be my opinion, but my opinion is that the first person files the patent, develops the technology, pays for the marketing, gets the buzz going to create brand awareness – and then somebody comes in and knocks it off, or waits for them to go out of business, and they make the money. Maybe they have better distribution. Maybe it's a company that is more established on a retail level, so they don't have to fight for space on shelves in a supermarket or a superstore. It's been my experience that unfortunately, crime pays in the inventing world.

Here's the downside to inventing. When you own Intellectual Property (IP) – patents, in particular, it is your responsibility to defend it. You must defend it or you will lose it. If you knowingly don't defend it, then you are giving permission to everyone to knock it off. All you get for defending a patent is what's known as treble damages, which equates to about a third of what you caught them with.

Here is a real example of what happened to me. Russell Sxxxxxxs knocked off one of my patents on a tattoo hang tag for a brand he called Pxxt Farm. I met with him; he looked me in the eyes and said, "Cute idea, kid, not for us." Six months later, it was on all of his garments. But he only did about $10,000 worth of business. It cost me $25,000 to hire a lawyer and to have letters and FedExes sent that he never even opened. He played it right. You just don't respond. But it was basically the breaking of my inventing back. I learned that inventing is really a rich man's game, which I wasn't, so I was done. Just between that and the arguments with the Patent Office, I was so turned off to it all. Other inventors could be, too. Who knows what products we'll never see because life beats the confidence out of them?

Inventing is expensive. Make sure you are in it for real and it's not just a hobby or an ego stroke. Make sure you are properly financed for the long haul and have a plan. I know of no overnight success and I've done this most my life and not everyone has the stomach for this. I didn't.

Let's do a little more of a deep dive into patents – just in case you want to pursue them. You might begin by asking, when is it wise to apply for a patent and when is it unwise to patent? Here's what I've learned. Let's start with some data: every day 1,700 patent applications are submitted. There are now approximately 8,000 examiners who review those patents. It is not easy to review a patent. There's a ton of research; there's a ton of technical talk. It is now taking five years for patents to issue, and they only last 20 years from filing date, roughly 15 years from issue date. That's not a lot of time for exclusivity. You also may not want your IP published for everyone to see. So some things to consider.

The mistake most inventors make is that they file early. By the time their product comes to market, they're already making something that isn't covered by their own patent. In my opinion, there are other ways of protecting the fort – trademarks, distribution, copyrights, trade secrets, are all wonderful tools. Patents can still work. Design patents make no sense. They only last eight years and they're easy to get around, but utility patents are gold. Utility patents have some great value; they last a long time, 20 years from filing. If you can file additional patents near the end of the life of your original patent that extend another 20 years, that's a good plan – staggering the filings. When does a patent make sense? When it's too big of an idea for the inventor, and he or she wants to license it or do something bigger than they can do themselves. You still need to apply for the patent because you have to have the number in order to license it. Consider this: investors are in love with the idea of patents, whether they always make sense or not because there's a tangible thing of value. They need to own a percentage of patent number 55555222xyz. That's another example of why you need it.

A final thought about applying for your patents. The advantage I had was working with a lawyer who was outside of Baltimore, close to Washington. We went down and met with the examiner. The way the process works, at least then, is you file your patent. Then they come back and reject you and say, here are your 24 points, 18 of them are approved, six of them are not. Then you can accept it with the 18 but you want the other six. We would then start the paper trail fights. Eventually we would just book an appointment, go down to the patent office, meet with the examiner and explain how the invention works. Then they see that it makes sense, and they approve it. They're very nice. They're just overworked. This was in the early 1990s. Back then they were still using paper files; they weren't digital. Also, lawyers in the Washington area are cheaper than New York, for example.

Here's an excellent example. A young kid some years ago had an idea for a piece of luggage of a different design. I referred him to somebody who already was in that business. I said, you don't have the wherewithal; you don't have the means of manufacturing, distribution, or capitalization. She does; license it to her.

I came up with an idea that I never did anything with. I remember taking a shower one morning – my wife at the time always wanted me to squeegee the shower doors after every shower – and it suddenly hit me: Why can't they squeegee themselves? All of a sudden, I jumped out of the shower with only a towel on. I went running down to the car and took the windshield wipers off of all the cars to figure out how to get the doors to squeegee themselves. It was too big an idea for me to break into the shower door industry. So, that had to be something to license. You have to then go to a shower door company and say we have an idea for a product for a self-squeegeeing shower door. That would be the only way something like that would see the light of day. You don't want to get into the cell phone tower business; you don't want to get into the automotive business. There are a lot of people out there who are happy to license good ideas.

Learning from my mistakes, I took my eye off the ball as to what got me to the point where I had the opportunity to keep creating as many inventors do. Shiny object syndrome, focusing on the next product. Don't do that. Instead, get your team in place and manage the system before moving on to the next idea. We also have to decide if it's just an idea or if it's really a business. There are advantages to both that your lawyer and accountant can discuss with you.

My loss is your gain. I've decided that as I know how to invent and create, and do it really well, that for me, at least, I am better off selling picks and shovels than looking for gold myself. So here is what I know about inventing and some of the tricks I have learned.

Here's how inventing works, with me at least. You can't plan for it, you can't say today I'm going to come up with my next great idea, you just have to recognize them when they happen and know what to do with it. Kind of perfect timing for this book and just part of how it all happens.

I am building a new city in the metaverse for my virtual trade shows and will now have a city experience with retail space, see how I did that? :-) I use a Mac with a trackpad and I am having a hard time getting the building to land and they are just hovering in space. I'll eventually just hire someone to build it, but I need to know how these things are done for editing reasons later when clients move in.

Anyway, I was looking at my desk and I always have my iPad with an iPen sitting next to my computer for taking meeting notes which I love to do, keeps me engaged and my notes are then searchable. It then occurred to me and for me inventing always comes from necessity. Why can't the iPad be a big track pad with many more options?

In today's inventing world I am able to do a quick search and found many products doing what I was looking for and purchased a Mobile Mouse app for $2.99. That saved me a ton of money, aggravation, and anxiety – and I got a new work toy.

This is how it used to work... Come up with the idea. Figure out the workings of it. Build a prototype, rebuild the prototype for mass production, trademark the name by flying it over as many states as we could,

Maine to San Diego, San Diego to Washington State, Washington to Florida and every state you flew over the trademark was considered in use. We then needed to hire a lawyer, file a patent application and wait and wait some more.... This would have cost about $25,000 and taken a good 18 months, now much, much longer as you will see later in these chapters.

In the old days we would have had to hire perhaps an engineer, a designer, an artist or others who could make sketches. We'd need to talk to manufacturers and of course lawyers and would be completely distracted with our better mouse trap.

Today we do a google search and can move on with our lives to our next idea and that's how the cookie can crumble and how it can work for inventors.

Chapter 1: What's the Why behind your invention?
We must first give credit to Simon Sinek for his inspirational TEDx talk "Start with why" where he refers to the question, "What's your why?" (Why do you do what you do?) What is the expression? Necessity is the mother of invention. Invention truly does come

from one's own needs, at least it did on some for me. My best idea to date were my medicated removable tattoos, Med-Tats™. This came to me when I couldn't get one of my kids to take her children's Tylenol® but could always get her to put on a tattoo. So why not put acetaminophen in the tattoos and have the image change as it was absorbed, which I did. That one cost me a home and a marriage. I'd do it again as it was my homerun shot, and I went for it. This is probably because I am an entrepreneur first and an inventor second. If I was an inventor who became a business owner, that's a bird of a different color.

That's another thing about inventors and entrepreneurs in general; we tend to go for it. We also know that there is a light at the end of the tunnel and just hope it's not a train coming at us, there better be.

You know the definition of insanity is doing the same thing over and over again and expecting different results. Well, much of our insanity is knowing exactly how a situation is going to play out and we do it anyway. I think that has something to do with inventing in general. So, by all means, know the why behind your what. Why are you taking the risk, why are you risking the money and embarrassment if it doesn't work out? The answer isn't just money. The answer needs to be something more. Your passion, your why, just know what it is and build from that. My why is that I am passionate about entrepreneurs' passion and just about everything I do professionally stems from that.

It's also important to know where ideas come from. For me at least, they come from an almost sleep state of mind as do many great ideas for many people. That's why people used to sleep with pen and paper by their bed. I used to do a lot of long-distance driving and the ideas would come when driving or when I was about to fall into a deep sleep. Maybe just be aware of some of your ideas when you are really tired. I feel like I already wrote this, but worth mentioning in case this is the only section you read. Albert Einstein used to take naps with a metal tray next to him and held two metal balls in his hands. This way when he hit REM sleep he'd drop the balls, which would hit the tray and wake him up; this prevented him from hitting REM sleep so he could be aware of the ideas flowing.

Why are you doing this? Why are you taking a shot? Why aren't you just staying on the safer roads getting a job and working for someone else versus venturing onto the roads less traveled with your ideas?

All inventions must serve a need of some type. If you have a better mouse trap it's to catch mice better, faster, cheaper, easier, cleaner, etc... What's your why? Why are you doing this? Not to make money; what's the real driving force that people can get behind? Necessity is truly the mother of all invention, but it's not the why and it's not why people buy.

Where do ideas come from? Why us? Can I do this?

Think about it. Why do people buy Nike® versus Adidas® or Puma® or Fila®? Why do people buy Apple® versus Dell® or HP® computers? What's your why?

Chapter 2: Inventing SOP, Standard Operating Procedures

Inventing is done a little differently now with the internet. You can easily do a first pass patent or trademark search on your own. In the old days we had to wait what could be months for searches to be done. You had to pay a lawyer $1,400 bucks to file a trademark and what you were paying for is the search. We can do a lot of that now on the internet. If you're not sure if your name is trademarked or not, go see if the domain is available. It's not foolproof, but you'll have a pretty good idea if the name is a domain, that someone is using it and has a ™ next to the name.

If all goes well, you will still need to have your lawyer do an in-depth search and it costs about $800 of your $1,200 for the initial ™ filing. You can learn a ton by just doing a Google® and/or GoDaddy® search. Sometimes, although not pleasant, you can find there are already 10 of your ideas out there, saving you a ton of money and embarrassment.

Second, come up with a name, a trademarkable name. Not like yellow pencil, that's descriptive, so it's not trademarkable. I love trademarks. They are quick, cheap, easy, and last forever. Coca-Cola® has done pretty well with just a trademark and a copyright and trade secret.

Come up with a great name, non-descriptive, but great. I am as proud of my trademarks as I am of my inventions. Just because they cost less doesn't mean they do less. In fact, they can do much more because they have a longer shelf life.

Depending on your idea, it's time to make a prototype. Think big here. Hopefully you will be filing for a utility patent which has partially to do with how your product is manufactured, so think mass market and please don't file your patent too early.

A utility patent protects the unique functionality of your invention, while a design patent only covers the physical look or ornamental appearance of your invention. A utility patent typically has to do with a manufacturing process. That's what makes them bulletproof. You describe what it does and its use and what it looks like, but it has nothing to do with the color, size, and shape. It has a lot to do with how it's made. That's always a part of it. However, that's not to say if you change the manufacturing process, that you won't be protected, but it is in the equation. The other type of patent is a process patent.

When should you file for a patent? Well, first you want to make a prototype. It's been my experience, you need to find somebody who's got an engineering, design, and manufacturing background to help you design the product in a way that it can be made for the mass market. Nobody's filing a patent to sell one or two of something. We all have these lofty goals of selling lots of these, and we're going to manufacture lots of these then, and the patent should be able to protect that. What a lot of inventors do is they file too early. And by the time the product comes out, it's already around their own patent, so they're no longer protected. We will explain this in a bit more detail later.

If you have to hire someone to build your working prototype, have them sign a non-disclosure agreement and understanding that they are engaged on a work for hire basis. That means they have no ownership of the invention.

You should have learned a lot by now. You should be more in love with your idea, not less. You should be thinking of pricing based on what you've learned from the prototype. Once you know your basic costs, you can figure out your selling price. In many industries, a keystone is the normal mark-up, which means doubling your production costs. If it costs you $5 to make it, we are selling it for $10 and it will probably retail at $20.

Now we can start shopping for lawyers. Talk to a few. Patent law is expensive. I once left a patent lawyer a voicemail and got a $550 invoice. That was the last message I left him, but that's what these lawyers get.

For me, what was important was having a lawyer near the patent office. As we mentioned in the introduction, it's never a bad idea to meet with the patent examiner, if you can. A lawyer with those types of relationships is great. Generally, when you file your patent the patent office will come back accepting maybe 18 of your 24 claims. That's why it helps to meet with them and discuss what wasn't accepted, if that's important to you. As we described earlier, you may even end up reversing some of the rejections.

You are going to need to think of financing. There, unfortunately, is a practical side to inventing and if you are banking everything on your great idea, you will probably run out of gas. I know that you will be told the process takes about a year. Ha! I've never had a patent issued in a year. I think my best was 14 months and that was for a design patent. You don't want those by the way. They get knocked off easily and only last eight years. Just an ego stroke, but you get to hang a plaque on your wall at least.

Part of the reason for having IP is to license or franchise or receive a royalty. Regardless of the medium, you will receive money from the license, but there needs to be an IP to do it with. So, license your patented product and the contract will be written up with the patent number. I am not sure what someone would be paying for if you weren't issued or had no IP, as there is no vehicle to license.

Now we need to find a manufacturer. Here are some things to consider. Who's going to be buying your product? Not necessarily the end consumer but the retailer, wholesaler, or other manufacturer, depending on what you sell. Where will you mainly be shipping to? In many situations your profit is in the buying, manufacturing, and shipping. Why not manufacture next to your biggest clients? Just a thought.

As you read earlier, my first invention was a hangtag in the apparel industry, Tattoo Hangtags® to be exact. Back then most of the garments were coming in from China so I needed to find a Chinese manufacturer. I needed to be able to sample in the U.S. and ship from China to anywhere in the world. With the help of some great domestic artists, Jason Kamps and Barry Jabloner, I was able to make mock samples domestically and then ship production from China to anywhere in the world.

Next, I needed to find a shipping vendor / partner, someone who could private-label ship for me. Meaning, take what the manufacturer had made and put everything in our own labeled boxes with our shipping papers. That's another key relationship to have in place.

Now we just need orders, business, or clients.

The Three Feet of Distribution

There is an essential three feet when inventing. We need to get ideas from your head to your pocket in the form of money. How are you going to do that? A WEBSITE IS NOT THE ONLY ANSWER!!!

A website is part of the answer perhaps, but not the end all and if it is, how are you going to support it? HOW ARE YOU GETTING YOUR PRODUCT OR SERVICE TO CONSUMERS? This is perhaps your most important IP there is and is generally overlooked. Distribution is key and where the focus should be once you've protected your fort with IP and figured out safe and reliable manufacturing. These relationships are key and ones where you can't get knocked off. Know your buyers, cherish them, protect them, take care of them, and they will take care of you.

Understanding what the supply chain is in an industry is important too. For example, in the automotive aftermarket there's a whole set of steps. It goes from the manufacturer to what's called a WD, a warehouse distributor, down to a sub distributor, and then down to a jobber who then sells it to the local retailer or garage, and then to the consumer.

You need to understand the rules of supermarkets and of the mega stores like the Walmart®s of the world. When it comes to supermarkets in particular, they don't make their money just on food. They make their money on slotting allowances – people are paying for the shelf space. They're paying for the ad in the circular. They're paying for the announcements in store. They're paying for that shelf talker that hangs off the shelf; they're paying for that floor display and the endcap display.

Most important, if it doesn't sell many times, you have to essentially buy it back. One of the large chain drug stores was led to believe that the vendor was going to invest a million dollars in advertising to support a new product. The company didn't run the advertising, and everything got shipped back at their expense. They use what they call velocity reports, where they're counting the number of times a product turns over. If it doesn't turn fast enough, they throw your product off the shelves. To the chain store, that shelf space is worth a lot of money. In that case, the vendor is paying the shipping both ways and the packaging both ways.

You also need to think about your displays, how things are going to look and be packaged, and whether the customer can figure out how to open it. You're not going to go to 10,000 stores and do it, so you're relying on a minimum wage employee to put together your product. In addition to that, with the retail chains, you have to be aware of planograms unless you're doing a floor type display, like in Costco®. Otherwise, you're talking about at least six months out before you can even get your product onto the shelves. Distribution is such a vital part of your success.

Sometimes you have to outmaneuver your competition when it comes to distribution. Here is an example of where that became critical. A Chinese company that was manufacturing umbrellas for department store chains decided to license the London Fog® name. Everybody knows London Fog® and you associate the name with rain wear. But in fact, London Fog® didn't make umbrellas. They only made raincoats. So, they went into the department stores and Totes®, their major competitor, came in and knocked them out. They said to the department stores, we'll give you the gloves and the hats and the coats and the overshoes and the umbrellas all – take the whole line and you will get 5% off the top. And they knocked London Fog® out. What London Fog® did was to use alternative distribution routes. Instead of department stores, they went into office superstores and places like that.

That was pre-internet. Back then, catalogs might have been a place you could also do that. Distribution is king. Years ago, there was a Sears® catalog. That was the Amazon® of the world. You could get anything and everything in the Sears® catalog from socks and kitchen tools to skateboards and even houses. You would just start dreaming when you're going through it. Now it's the internet; now it's Amazon®. We don't know what it's going to be next but that it's all about distribution. To be higher versus lower on the shelf becomes important, as well. You need to work with people who understand this. You need to realize that you can't do it all yourself.

Pricing - I touched on this briefly a moment ago. A way of pricing is by keystoning it, doubling your manufacturing costs. Remember, you have a patented product, an exclusive, so you can kind of name your price, but it's generally a good practice to make your product as reasonably priced so you get business.

A suggestion that I like in determining prices is to work it backwards. Know your market. Know what a fair price would be and start working it from there.

Let's say you have a new, more humane, better, faster, cleaner mouse trap. See what the current prices are that people are paying for mouse traps and if you can make the profit margin you want in that range. Keep in mind that the retailers, if you are going that route, are going to need to make their money as well, generally a keystone again. So, if your mouse trap is going to retail for $20. That means you need to offer it to the retailers at $10 landed, manufacture it at $5 FOB your manufacturing facility, leaving you $5. You then have to figure out if that's enough and what volume you need to sell to support you, your team, your lifestyle, and whatever else.

There are always going to be expenses you didn't think of so give yourself some buffer. These are basic numbers, not for all products or all industries. I only had one that made it to retail – Whozy Woozy®, gemstone tattoos – and didn't do very well.

Sales

By now you are patent pending, which means you have a filing date. YOU DON'T HAVE TO WAIT FOR YOUR PATENT TO ISSUE TO START SELLING OR TAKING ORDERS. Patent Pending, in my opinion, is your best time. You have a filing date and are protected. You aren't published, so no one can knock you off by seeing how you are manufacturing. You can get press for filing and show trusted clients what you've got. You can add some time with a provisional patent application, which your lawyer can explain, but you can get a full 20 years of protection versus 17 years.

Last, and somewhat obvious, is that you have to be able to deliver. I am not going to tell you how to run your business – well I guess I am. Why go through all of this if you aren't going to come through with what you've promised?

Then read my other book, *On The Bus™ WorkBook*, on how to sell better or hire me as a consultant, but you are pretty much there.

So, to review...

1. Do a search
2. Come up with a great name
3. Make a prototype
4. Get a great lawyer

5. Figure out your financing

6. Figure out your manufacturing

7. Figure out your distribution and packaging

8. Figure out your pricing

9. Figure out your sales

10. Figure out your on-time delivery

Easy, right? No overnight successes, right; do the work.

Chapter 3: Basic Mistakes

Some basic mistakes that inventors make:

- Getting too excited, *telling everyone or writing a book sharing all of your trade secrets, yes we are protected*.
- Not protecting the fort.
- Being so paranoid that you don't tell *anyone*.
- Not going through the previously mentioned Inventing SOP.
- Filing too narrow of a description. I think I've got a dozen patented products on two or three of my patents, so bigger is better here with your filing.

Stick with manufacturing facts, more so than with use. That's where you can get pigeonholed. Let's elaborate on that a bit. When filing any utility patent, you could have multiple uses, so I tell people I have a dozen patented products. But the reality is, I think I only have five or six patents but some of the patents have multiple uses. Stick to the manufacturing process in your filing, because that's what the examiners will look at, more so than your use. For example, a cup could be used to drink out of, but it could also be used to hold pens, so they don't need to know that. They need to know that you're making a round object made out of a certain material that has a handle and how you're making it. That is more important than what the end user will use it for. If you get bogged down in the use, they're going to limit the scope of your patent and that gives them the opportunity to say, no, you can't do this, you can't do that, because somebody else does. Don't tell them. Tell them what you're making and how you're making it and a brief idea of what it's for perhaps.

The biggest mistake is filing too early. You will end up knocking off your own patent. Think about this: The more you do this, the more prototypes you make, the more ideas that you get from the outside from your manufacturers, or whomever it might be – you're tweaking your product. Don't file until you're done tweaking. You may also find out it's least expensive to use an adhesive versus a staple, let's say. Well, that's a major difference in your patent. If you're going to use an adhesive instead of a staple, or tape or whatever it might be, that's a manufacturing process right there. You need to stop tweaking and then file.

Chapter 4: Protect the Fort

This is really your lawyer's job to guide you on. I liked having a lawyer near the patent office for the reason we stated before. In case you need to go and sit down with the patent examiner, it's a little easier if they are local.

Part of protecting the fort is defending your IP, intellectual property. This is a must. Once you've allowed someone to knock off your idea knowingly without defending it you've now allowed everyone to do it. So be aggressive here and maybe try to license vs. prosecute turning a bad situation into a good one.

I've learned from writing this book, as I've laid out how we do things, that I must now file a utility patent and rely heavily on the Copyright as I've given away our trade secrets as I am disclosing our processes. So I'll be filing in the next 12 months. So be warned what's in here is my property and I'd have no choice but to defend it.

There are many ways of protecting your product, your fort, some better than others. Do you really need a patent, trademark, copyright, or trade secret? What are the responsibilities of owning these types of IP?

I am not a lawyer or even a Patent Agent, but I have some experience here and opinions. Get a lawyer, don't wing this part. Just know that part of creating and protecting your IP is defending it. You must defend your IP, which is expensive, but legally you must defend it or you are allowing everyone else to use it. So think it through and run it by your support people.

Patents – and there are several types – are typically for protecting inventions of products, processes, changes to existing products, manufacturing procedures, and formulas that perhaps are no longer trade secrets.

Trade Secrets – These are just that, trade secrets: Recipes, formulas, process, the unique way you do things.

Tradmark – These are your names, which cannot be descriptive. As mentioned earlier you can not ™ a yellow pencil, calling it a yellow pencil, but here's a type you probably could use: The Original Yellow Pencil™. Here's another type, a ™ means that at some point in the future you will be filing for a ©. You don't need a lawyer to start using a ™ if you believe the name is unique and you are planning on registering it soon.

Copyright – This protects creative work, books, albums, articles, greeting cards, directions, and all the information in this book...

My favorite type of IP isn't even IP, but such a valuable part of the equation I hope you will treat it that way: distribution. Maybe all you need is distribution. I remember coaching a battery company with an exclusive relationship with a big box store based on a handshake that lasted decades. This was great until they wanted to sell the business and it wasn't easy without an exclusive contract.

Distribution can come in many forms, but in short it's taking your idea from your head to your pocket and you might consider:

> Licensing
>
> Franchising
>
> Distributors
>
> Doing it all yourself

For me a focus is more on the 27 inches it takes to get an idea from your head to your pocket in the form of money in your pocket. Distribution is typically relationship-based and something that you can't just knock off, steal, or copy. Work on your relationships with your manufacturers, customers, and vendors. I was recently accused of being someone who harbors relationships. I hope that's a good thing, probably an accurate thing.

Cost of entry is another. Dies and molds are very expensive and can keep some people out of industries.

Patents, as we discussed, come in a number of different types:

> Design patent – I have one of these for a plush doll I developed. These last about eight years and are

really just an ego stroke as they are easy to knock off. Change a color, size, or style and you're around it.

Utility Patents – covered in Chapter 2

Owning IP is a responsibility. You must sue so that lawyers are typically the only ones making money.

Chapter 5: The Concept

For me, the process is coming up with the idea, figuring out if there's a need for it, figuring out how to go about making it, and what it would look like, and then figuring out how to make it on a mass production level. You need to go through all of that. Then you've got to figure out the pricing. You know, it's one thing if you can make it for $20. But if the market is only going to bear $1.50, why proceed? You need to figure out how to make it for a quarter. Those factors are all part of it.

Where does it come from? For me so many of my ideas have come when in a sleep state of mind. Driving long distances, when you are one eyeing it, has been a time for me, pay attention to your thoughts. This used to happen when I was commuting from

Maryland to NY on Tuesdays and Thursdays, four hours each way, I'd come up with some great stuff. Remember Albert Einstein sleeping with metal balls in his hands and a metal tray next to him so he'd wake up just when he was in that creative state. That's kind of the brilliant being brilliant, knowing themselves or, as I like to say, I've been me for a long time and know me pretty well. I am no Einstein, but he knew himself pretty well, too.

Many times in the trades, dentists, chefs, doctors, trainers, we come up with products from necessity. I can say that with Med-Tats™ as I needed a way of getting my daughter to take her fever medicine.

Just beware, many times the first person in the invention chain loses money, generally, but not always. Others are looking to knock them off. Again, a lot of this is my opinion, but it's based on my own inventing experiences that sometimes it's the second person who makes money as the originator runs out of gas.

Chapter 6: What To Do When You Have a Product Idea

Today we get to do things a little differently, Google it.

See what's out there already.

Design it in your mind.

Figure out the need and who the audience is.

Think about pricing and profit.

Chapter 7: Making a Prototype

If you are making a product, then you need to make the product fully. Prototypes are fine, drawings probably not, but then we need to file as a drawing. Let me explain. If you are making a new kind of drone, let's say, you need to make the drone or at least have a model of some type of it. You will need to file in a drawing form, but it's imperative that you build it. You will learn so much from building it both in a prototype form while always thinking of mass production.

Chapter 8: Building Your Team

Remember it's your team. If you want to look forward to Mondays and be excited about people visiting your office, you better like your team. It doesn't matter how good someone may be, if you don't like them it will strain the relationship and prevent you from being creative.

I only want positive energy around me. I don't want to waste my energy with negativity.

Picking Lawyers - I've talked about the importance of a lawyer. Find one you can talk to without the meter running. Learn what you can from lawyers. Remember they aren't judges, but lawyers can guide you. For Intellectual Property type of law, I like lawyers near the USPTO, or at least ones that have relationships there. Just don't try to do it alone, there is a lot to be said for a lawyer's education, experience, and knowledge.

Picking Manufacturers - This is a key relationship. Treasure it. They will determine your pricing, delivery, inventory, and everything unless you want to do it in house. Communication is key. Manage your vendors.

Picking Partners - If you have to have a partner make sure that you have defined roles and time that will be invested by each. You probably shouldn't both be strong in the same area. Make sure also you are on the same page for exiting. Get key employee insurance on each other.

Picking Artists - Artists for creative types are important if you don't have that skill. I find that I need someone who can get in my head and take what I am thinking and put it on my screen without too many attempts. If you can find that, that's gold. I've found those types of artists a few times and one who can even take my visions a step further which has its pluses and minuses.

I sure hope this book helps you. Writing it helped me, now it's yours. Use it, share it, live it, love it. It works if you work it...

- Chris Lipper

About The Author

I am privileged to have done a lot in my professional life. Prior to On The Bus™ I was a professional inventor for 15 years in a multiple of industries. I had a brief management roll with both Radio Shack and LensCrafters and represented a number of companies in the apparel industry. I've founded five companies and sold advertising and had my Series 7 on Wall Street when I was 20 years old. So I've done a lot and worked with and for all types of owners. I consider this manuscript my life's work and hope you enjoyed it. If you ever want to discuss any of it or know someone who could benefit from what we do, please schedule time wtih me at www.onthebus.biz.

Chris Lipper is also the author of *On The Bus™ Sales Training WorkBook* ©2021.

www.ingramcontent.com/pod-product-compliance
Lightning Source LLC
Chambersburg PA
CBHW062123020426
42335CB00013B/1081